28

Achieving

MCAS

Success in
ENGLISH
LANGUAGE
ARTS

HOWARD I. BERRENT, Ph.D.

Mc Graw Hill **Wright Group**

The **McGraw·Hill** Companies

Editor: Rebecca Grober

Executive Editor: Linda Kwil

Production Coordinator: Linda Chandler

Photo Researcher: Barb Gamache

Marketing Manager: Sheila Caswell

Cover Design: Tracey Harris-Sainz

Interior Design: Think Design Group LLC

Wright Group

ISBN: 0-07-704411-8

Send all inquiries to:
Wright Group/McGraw-Hill
130 East Randolph Street, Suite 400
Chicago, IL 60601

Printed in the United States of America

1 2 3 4 5 6 7 8 9 10 POH 08 07 06 05

Table of Contents

Acknowledgments

Excerpt on pages 20–22 from "Outlasting the Dinosaurs, An Interview with Dr. James Perran Ross", *Crocodiles*, www.pbs.org. Copyright © 2000 WGBH/Boston. Reprinted with permission from WGBH Educational Foundation.

Excerpt on pages 25–27 from *The Glass Menagerie* by Tennessee Williams. Copyright © 1945 The University of The South. Reprinted by permission of Georges Borchardt, Inc. for the Tennessee Williams Estate.

Excerpt on page 32 from "Inside Mexico: A peasant's life" by Ian Campbell, *United Press International*, June 23, 2003. Reprinted by permission of United Press International.

Excerpt on pages 36–37 from "China's Age of Invention", *Secrets of Lost Empires: China Bridge*, www.pbs.org. Copyright © 2000 WGBH/Boston. Reprinted with permission from WGBH Educational Foundation.

Excerpt on pages 41–42 from "The Airmail Bowling Ball" from *Saint Maybe* by Anne Tyler. Copyright © 1991 by Anne Tyler. Reprinted by permission of Alfred A. Knopf, a division of Random House, Inc. and Penguin Group (Canada), a Division of Pearson Penguin Canada Inc.

Poem on page 46 is "Neither Out Far Nor In Deep" from *The Poetry of Robert Frost* edited by Edward Connery Lathem. Copyright 1969 by Henry Holt and Company. Copyright 1936 by Robert Frost, copyright 1964 by Lesley Frost Ballantine. Reprinted by permission of Henry Holt and Company, LLC.

Poem on page 47 is "Design" from *The Poetry of Robert Frost* edited by Edward Connery Lathem. Copyright 1969 by Henry Holt and Company. Copyright 1936 by Robert Frost, copyright 1964 by Lesley Frost Ballantine. Reprinted by permission of Henry Holt and Company, LLC.

Excerpt on pages 51–52 from *The House on Mango Street*. Copyright © 1984 by Sandra Cisneros. Published by Vintage Books, a division of Random House, Inc., and in hardcover by Alfred A. Knopf in 1994. Reprinted by permission of Susan Bergholz Literary Services, New York. All rights reserved.

Excerpt on page 62 from "Old as the Trees in Niagara", *Environment*, May 2001, Vol. 43, No. 4, p. 6. Reprinted with permission of the Helen Dwight Reid Educational Foundation. Published by Heldref Publications, 1319 Eighteenth St., NW, Washington, DC 20036-1802. Copyright © 2001.

Excerpt on pages 66–67 from " Kingdom of Coral" by Douglas H. Chadwick, *National Georgraphic*, January 2001, Vol. 199, No. 1, p. 30. Reprinted by permission of the National Geographic Society.

Short Story on pages 71–72 is "Forget crackers - what Polly wants is a vacation", by Daniel Pinkwater, originally appeared in *Smithsonian*, October 1994. Reprinted by permission of the author.

Essay on pages 75–77 is "Founding Father's Right Touch; Word Whiz: Thomas Jefferson topped his works with Declaration of Independence", by Michael Mink, *Investor's Business Daily*, July 7, 2003. © 2003 Investor's Business Daily, Inc. Reprinted with permission. You may not copy, modify, redistribute, or display these material without the written consent of Investor's Business Daily. Investor's Business Daily and its licensors expressly disclaim any express or implied warranties or representations regarding the accuracy, completeness, timeliness, or reliability of information, facts, views, opinions or recommendations contained in this publication.

Article on page 82 is "Golden Girl" by Laura Daily, *National Geographic World*, February 2001, p. 10. Reprinted by permission of the National Geographic Society.

Excerpt on pages 85–86 from "The No Guitar Blues" from *Baseball in April and Other Stories* , copyright © 1990 by Gary Soto, reprinted by permission of Harcourt, Inc.

Excerpt on pages 89–90 from "The Mighty Conestoga" by Lisa Mullins Bishop, *Early American Homes*, August 1997, Vol. 28, No. 4, p. 16. Copyright © 1997, 2003, Firelands Media Group LLC, Early American Life Magazine. Reprinted by permission.

Article on page 94 is "Sea otter plan praised after delay", by Don Thompson, *Capper's*, April 29, 2003, Vol. 125, No. 9, p. 19. Used with permission of The Associated Press. Copyright © 2005. All rights reserved.

Excerpt on pages 98–99 from "Men At Work" from *Thinking Out Loud* by Anna Quindlen, 1993. Reprinted by permission of Random House Inc.

Excerpt on pages 103–104 from "I Stand Here Ironing", *Tell Me A Riddle* by Tillie Olsen, Dell Publishing, 1961. Reprinted by permission of the Elaine Markson Literary Agency.

Excerpt on page 108 from *Of Mice and Men* by John Steinbeck, copyright 1937, renewed © 1965 by John Steinbeck. Used by permission of Viking Penguin, a division of Penguin Group (USA), Inc.

Short Story on pages 112–113 is "A Conversation with My Father" from *Enormous Changes at the Last Minute* by Grace Paley. Copyright © 1971, 1974 by Grace Paley. Reprinted by permission of Farrar, Straus & Giroux, LLC.

Excerpt on page 126 from "The Rocking-Horse Winner", copyright 1933 by the Estate of D.H. Lawrence, renewed © 1961 by Angelo Ravagli and C.M. Weekley, Executors of the Estate of Frieda Lawrence, from *Complete Short Stories of D.H. Lawrence* by D.H. Lawrence. Used by permission of Viking Penguin, division of Penguin Group (USA) Inc.

Excerpt on pages 130–131 from "Good Country People" in *A Good Man is Hard to Find and Other Stories*, copyright © 1955 by Flannery O'Connor and renewed 1983 by Regina O'Conor, reprinted by permission of Harcourt, Inc.

Excerpt on pages 135–136 from "Night Before Battle" from *The Complete Short Stories of Ernest Hemingway*. Copyright 1939 by Esquire, Inc. Copyright renewed © 1967 by John Hemingway, Patrick Hemingway, and Gregory Hemingway. Reprinted with permission of Scribner, an imprint of Simon & Schuster Adult Publishing Group.

Excerpt on pages 157 from "The Sound of a Voice", *FOB and Other Plays* by David Henry Hwang. © David Henry Hwang. Reprinted by permission of the author.

Excerpt on pages 160–161 from Act I of *Pygmalion* by George Bernard Shaw. Reprinted by permission of The Society of Authors on behalf of the Bernard Shaw Estate.

Poem on pages 163–164 is "Filling Station" from *The Complete Poems: 1927-1979* by Elizabeth Bishop. Copyright © 1979, 1983 by Alice Helen Methfessel. Reprinted by permission of Farrar, Straus & Giroux, LLC.

Excerpt on pages 166–167 from *The Gap* by Eugène Ionesco, translated by Rosette C. Lamont. Reprinted by permission from *The Massachusetts Review*, Volume 10, Number 01, Summer, 1969.

Excerpt on page 172 from "Flying sharks: powerful hunters of false bay" by David George Gordon, *National Geographic Kids*, May 2004, p. 18. Reprinted by permission of the National Geographic Society.

Article on pages 175–177 is "'Inverted Jenny' Stamps On Display at National Postal Museum in D.C." by Scott McCaffrey, July 29, 1996. Copyright 2004, Knight Ridder/Tribune News Services. Reprinted with permission.

Excerpt on pages 180–181 from "The mountain goat foments trouble in a fragile paradise", by Charles Bergman, originally appeared in *Smithsonian*, August 1984. Reprinted by permission of the author.

Excerpt on page 184 from *Sounder* by William H. Armstrong. Text copyright © 1969 by William H. Armstrong. Used by permission of HarperCollins Publishers.

Excerpt on pages 226–228 from "Hurricanes of History - From Dinosaur Times to Today" by Willie Drye, *National Geographic News*, June 7, 2004. Reprinted by permission of the National Geographic Society.

To the Student

Introduction to the Grade 10 MCAS in English Language Arts

The Grade 10 MCAS English Language Arts Test is given in two parts:

- a Composition Test based on a writing prompt
- a Language and Literature Test with multiple-choice and open-response questions

The Composition Test will test your ability to create a piece of writing based on a writing prompt. The prompt will ask you to explain a specific idea using a work of literature you have read. You will write the composition on one day, separated into two sessions. During the first session, you will write a draft. After a short break, you will be given a longer time to revise the draft and present a final composition. This composition will be graded according to the MCAS Writing Scoring Guide for Grade 10.

The Language and Literature Test contains three separate parts, or sessions. You will take Sessions 1 and 2 on one day with a short break in between. Session 3 will be given the following day. The test will consist of reading passages taken from a variety of literary selections such as short stories, editorials, novel excerpts, interviews, poetry, plays, newspaper articles, and essays. In total, the Language and Literature Test contains 36 multiple-choice questions and 4 open-response questions. The multiple-choice questions require you to choose a correct answer from four options. Open-response questions require that you write a short paragraph answer. Your answer will be graded using a rubric that is designed for that individual question. You will need to show use of standard English as you answer the content of the question.

Objectives Tested on the Grade 10 MCAS in English Language Arts

There are 15 learning standards assessed in the lessons presented in this book:

Standard 4

Students will acquire and use correctly an advanced reading vocabulary of English words, identifying meanings through an understanding of word relationships.

4.23 Identify and use correctly idioms, cognates, words with literal and figurative meanings, and patterns of word changes that indicate different meanings or functions.

4.24 Use knowledge of Greek, Latin, or Norse mythology, the Bible, and other works alluded to in British and American literature to understand the meaning of new words.

4.25 Use general dictionaries, specialized dictionaries, thesauruses, or related references as needed to increase learning.

Standard 5

Students will identify, describe, and apply knowledge of the structure of the English language and standard English conventions for sentence structure, usage, punctuation, capitalization, and spelling.

5.23 Identify simple, compound, complex, and compound-complex sentences.

5.24 Identify nominalized, adjectival, and adverbial clauses.

5.25 Recognize the functions of verbals: participles, gerunds, and infinitives.

5.26 Analyze the structure of a sentence.

5.27 Identify rhetorically functional sentence structure (parallelism, properly placed modifiers).

5.28 Identify correct mechanics (semicolons, colons, hyphens), correct usage (tense consistency), and correct sentence structure (parallel structure).

5.29 Describe the origins and meanings of common words and foreign words or phrases used frequently in written English, and show their relationship to historical events or developments.

Standard 8

Students will decode accurately and understand new words encountered in their reading materials, drawing on a variety of strategies as needed, and then use these words accurately in . . . writing.

8.29 Identify and analyze patterns of imagery or symbolism.

8.30 Identify and interpret themes and give supporting evidence from a text.

8.31 Analyze the logic and use of evidence in an author's argument.

Standard 9

Students will identify the basic facts and essential ideas in what they have read, heard, or viewed.

9.6 Relate a literary work to primary source documents of its literary period or historical setting.

Standard 10

Students will identify, analyze, and apply knowledge of the characteristics of different genres.

10.5 Compare and contrast the presentation of a theme or topic across genres to explain how the selection of genre shapes the message.

Standard 11

Students will identify, analyze, and apply knowledge of theme in literature and provide evidence from the text to support their understanding.

11. 5 Apply knowledge of the concept that the theme or meaning of a selection represents a view or comment on life, and provide support from the text for the identified themes.

Standard 12

Students will identify, analyze, and apply knowledge of the structure and elements of fiction and provide evidence from the text to support their understanding.

12.5 Locate and analyze such elements in fiction as point of view, foreshadowing, and irony.

Standard 13

Students will identify, analyze, and apply knowledge of the structure, elements, and meaning of nonfiction or informational material and provide evidence from the text to support their understanding.

13.24 Analyze the logic and use of evidence in an author's argument.

13.25 Analyze and explain the structure and elements of nonfiction works.

Standard 14

Students will identify, analyze, and apply knowledge of the structure, elements, and theme of poetry and provide evidence from the text to support their understanding.

14.5 Identify, respond to, and analyze the effects of sound, form, figurative language, graphics, and dramatic structure of poems:

- sound (alliteration, onomatopoeia, rhyme scheme, consonance, assonance)

- form (ballad, sonnet, heroic couplets)

- figurative language (personification, metaphor, simile, hyperbole, symbolism)

- dramatic structure

Standard 15

Students will identify and analyze how an author's choice of words appeals to the senses, creates imagery, suggests mood, and sets tone.

15.7 Evaluate how an author's choice of words advances the theme or purpose of a work.

15.8 Identify and describe the importance of sentence variety in the overall effectiveness of an imaginary/literary or informational/ expository work.

Standard 17

Students will identify, analyze, and apply knowledge of the themes, structure, and elements of drama and provide evidence from the text to support their understanding.

17.7 Identify and analyze how dramatic conventions support, interpret, and enhance dramatic text.

Standard 19

Students will write compositions with a clear focus, logically related ideas to develop it, and adequate detail.

Standard 20

Students will select and use appropriate genres, modes of reasoning, and speaking styles when writing for different audiences and rhetorical purposes.

Standard 21

Students will demonstrate improvement in organization, content, paragraph development, level of detail, style, tone and word choice (diction) in their compositions after revising them.

Standard 22

Students will use knowledge of standard English conventions to edit their writing.

How to Use This Book

The Diagnostic Pretest

The book contains a pretest, lessons based on the Massachusetts objectives, and a posttest. The first thing you should do is take the pretest. Cut the Pretest Answer Booklet (pages 235–244) out of the back of your book and use it to record all of your answers.

Lesson and Reviews

The lessons cover 15 of the standards that appear on the Grade 10 MCAS English Language Arts exam. Before the lesson begins, the standard is stated and briefly explained.

Each lesson is divided into three steps:

Step One: Sample Passage and Questions
Read a short passage and the sample questions to follow. For the sample questions, explanations are given for each answer choice.

Step Two: Sidebar Instruction
Read a slightly longer passage and answer questions with the help of hints, called sidebars, in the margins.

Step Three: On Your Own
Read a full-length passage and answer the questions on your own.

With each step, the length and readability level of the passage increases. By step three, the passage is full-length and written at the 10th grade level. The lessons are designed to increase your endurance for reading longer passages and to slowly increase the level of difficulty.

Review

At the end of every three lessons is a review. The selections in the review are written at the 10th grade level and have questions based on the objectives covered in the previous lessons.

The Diagnostic Posttest

After you have completed all of the lessons and review, remove the Posttest Answer Booklet (pages 245–254) from the back of your book and take the posttest. After your teacher has scored the posttest, he or she can tell you if there are standards you need to review. Go back and redo the lessons related to those objectives.

Pretest

COMPOSITION

WRITING PROMPT

Characters in books are sometimes very different from ordinary people. They may have ideas that differ from those considered acceptable in society. They might dress and act differently.

From a work of literature you have read in or out of school, select a character that, in your opinion, is different from those around him or her. In a well-developed composition, identify that character and what makes him or her different.

Pages 2 and 3 are for your rough draft. Final copy should be written on pages 237 and 238 in your Student Answer Booklet.

English Language Arts
LANGUAGE AND LITERATURE: SESSION 1

DIRECTIONS

This session contains two reading selections and one poem with seventeen multiple-choice questions and two open-response questions. Mark your answers to these questions in the spaces provided in your Student Answer Booklet (page 239).

On January 20, 1961, John F. Kennedy became the thirty-fifth President of the United States. Though he was killed two years later, Kennedy proved to be one of America's greatest presidents. He worked to overcome some of the biggest challenges in the nation's history. These included the threat of nuclear war between the United States and the Soviet Union, and the dismal civil rights situation in America.

On his inauguration day, Kennedy made the following address.

from

John F. Kennedy's Inaugural Address

1   . . . The world is very different now. For man holds in his mortal hands the power to abolish all forms of human poverty and all forms of human life. And yet the same revolutionary beliefs for which our forebears* fought are still at issue around the globe—the belief that the rights of man come not from the generosity of the state, but from the hand of God.

2   We dare not forget today that we are the heirs of that first revolution. Let the word go forth from this time and place, to friend and foe alike, that the torch has been passed to a new generation of Americans—born in this century, tempered by war, disciplined by a hard and bitter peace, proud of our ancient heritage—and unwilling to witness or permit the slow undoing of those human rights to which this Nation has always been committed, and to which we are committed today at home and around the world.

3   Let every nation know, whether it wishes us well or ill, that we shall pay any price, bear any burden, meet any hardship, support

any friend, oppose any foe, in order to assure the survival and the success of liberty.

4   This much we pledge—and more.

5   To those old allies whose cultural and spiritual origins we share, we pledge the loyalty of faithful friends. United, there is little we cannot do in a host of cooperative ventures. Divided, there is little we can do—for we dare not meet a powerful challenge at odds and split asunder.

6   To those new States whom we welcome to the ranks of the free, we pledge our word that one form of colonial control shall not have passed away merely to be replaced by a far more iron tyranny. We shall not always expect to find them supporting our view. But we shall always hope to find them strongly supporting their own freedom—and to remember that, in the past, those who foolishly sought power by riding the back of the tiger ended up inside.

7   To those peoples in the huts and villages across the globe struggling to break the bonds of mass misery, we pledge our best efforts to help them help themselves, for whatever period is required—not because the Communists may be doing it, not because we seek their votes, but because it is right. If a free society cannot help the many who are poor, it cannot save the few who are rich.

8   To our sister republics south of our border, we offer a special pledge—to convert our good words into good deeds—in a new alliance for progress—to assist free men and free governments in casting off the chains of poverty. But this peaceful revolution of hope cannot become the prey of hostile powers. Let all our neighbors know that we shall join with them to oppose aggression or subversion* anywhere in the Americas. And let every other power know that this Hemisphere intends to remain the master of its own house.

9   To that world assembly of sovereign states, the United Nations, our last best hope in an age where the instruments of war have far outpaced the instruments of peace, we renew our pledge of support—to prevent it from becoming merely a forum for invective*—to strengthen its shield of the new and the weak—and to enlarge the area in which its writ may run.

10   Finally, to those nations who would make themselves our adversary, we offer not a pledge but a request: that both sides begin anew the quest for peace, before the dark powers of destruction unleashed by science engulf all humanity in planned or accidental self-destruction.

11   We dare not tempt them with weakness. For only when our arms are sufficient beyond doubt can we be certain beyond doubt that they will never be employed.

12   But neither can two great and powerful groups of nations take comfort from our present course—both sides overburdened by the cost of modern weapons, both rightly alarmed by the steady spread of the deadly atom, yet both racing to alter that uncertain balance of terror that stays the hand of mankind's final war.

13   So let us begin anew—remembering on both sides that civility is not a sign of weakness, and sincerity is always subject to proof. Let us never negotiate out of fear. But let us never fear to negotiate.

14   Let both sides explore what problems unite us instead of belaboring those problems which divide us.

15   Let both sides, for the first time, formulate serious and precise proposals for the inspection and control of arms—and bring the absolute power to destroy other nations under the absolute control of all nations.

16   Let both sides seek to invoke the wonders of science instead of its terrors. Together let us explore the stars, conquer the deserts, eradicate disease, tap the ocean depths, and encourage the arts and commerce.

17   Let both sides unite to heed in all corners of the earth the command of Isaiah—to "undo the heavy burdens and to let the oppressed go free."

18   And if a beachhead of cooperation may push back the jungle of suspicion, let both

sides join in creating a new endeavor, not a new balance of power, but a new world of law, where the strong are just and the weak secure and the peace preserved.

19   All this will not be finished in the first one hundred days. Nor will it be finished in the first one thousand days, nor in the life of this Administration, nor even perhaps in our lifetime on this planet. But let us begin.

20   In your hands, my fellow citizens, more than in mine, will rest the final success or failure of our course. Since this country was founded, each generation of Americans has been summoned to give testimony to its national loyalty. The graves of young Americans who answered the call to service surround the globe.

21   Now the trumpet summons us again—not as a call to bear arms, though arms we need; not as a call to battle, though embattled we are—but a call to bear the burden of a long twilight struggle, year in and year out, "rejoicing in hope, patient in tribulation"—a struggle against the common enemies of man: tyranny, poverty, disease, and war itself.

22   Can we forge against these enemies a grand and global alliance, North and South, East and West, that can assure a more fruitful life for all mankind? Will you join in that historic effort?

23   In the long history of the world, only a few generations have been granted the role of defending freedom in its hour of maximum danger. I do not shrink from this responsibility—I welcome it. I do not believe that any of us would exchange places with any other people or any other generation. The energy, the faith, the devotion which we bring to this endeavor will light our country and all who serve it—and the glow from that fire can truly light the world.

24   And so, my fellow Americans: ask not what your country can do for you—ask what you can do for your country.

25   My fellow citizens of the world: ask not what America will do for you, but what together we can do for the freedom of man.

26   Finally, whether you are citizens of America or citizens of the world, ask of us the same high standards of strength and sacrifice which we ask of you. With a good conscience our only sure reward, with history the final judge of our deeds, let us go forth to lead the land we love, asking His blessing and His help, but knowing that here on earth God's work must truly be our own.

---

*forebears – founders
*subversion – corruption
*invective – hateful speech

1 According to Kennedy, what is different about the modern world?

A. People are able to educate themselves easily.

B. People are able to travel around the globe quickly, which makes war deadlier.

C. People have enough power to solve their problems or destroy themselves.

D. People have the knowledge and materials to build complex machines.

2 Read this line from the passage:

> Now the trumpet summons and is again—

In the sentence above, the word *summons* is used as

A. a conjunction.

B. a verb.

C. a preposition.

D. an adjective.

3 Which of these would Kennedy consider to be a poor use of scientific knowledge?

A. exploring the stars

B. tapping the ocean depths

C. eradicating disease

D. spying on friendly nations

4 According to Kennedy, what will be the final judge of a person's deeds?

A. the world assembly

B. the economy

C. history

D. monuments

5 In paragraph 24, what is one effect of the author saying, "Ask not what your country can do for you—ask what you can do for your country"?

A. It motivates people to fight Communists.

B. It encourages people to stop applying for money from the government.

C. It stresses the importance of acting generously and responsibly.

D. It illustrates the need to break new international records.

6 What is Kennedy's main point in paragraph 11?

A. America needs weapons to attack and defeat the Soviet Union.

B. America needs weapons for protection and security.

C. America needs to pretend they have less than they really do.

D. America needs to lure the Soviet Union into a trap.

7 In paragraph 12, Kennedy says the "deadly atom" has caused alarm. To what is he referring?

A. nuclear weapons

B. terrible fright

C. a Cold War

D. a disease epidemic

 8 Overall, what does Kennedy most want from the world?

A. support and funding

B. spy reports

C. war and weaponry

D. peace and cooperation

Write your answer to open-response question 9 in the space provided in your Student Answer Booklet.

 9 In his inaugural address, Kennedy used motivational language to encourage citizens to take action that would make the country and the world a better place. Identify at least three such examples and explain how each one was motivational. Use relevant and specific information from the article to support your answer.

H.G. Wells's famous 1898 novel The War of the Worlds *was a fictional account of America being invaded by Martian space aliens. In 1938, radio personality Orson Welles used the book as the basis for a radio drama. Unfortunately, many people mistook it for a news report. All across the nation, people panicked in the streets!*

In this selection, the narrator watches the Martian vehicles invading a city.

from

The War of the worlds

by H.G. Wells

1   After eating we crept back to the scullery*, and there I must have dozed again, for when presently I looked round I was alone. The thudding vibration continued with wearisome persistence. I whispered for the curate* several times, and at last felt my way to the door of the kitchen. It was still daylight, and I perceived him across the room, lying against the triangular hole that looked out upon the Martians. His shoulders were hunched, so that his head was hidden from me.

2   I could hear a number of noises almost like those in an engine shed; and the place rocked with that beating thud. Through the aperture in the wall I could see the top of a tree touched with gold and the warm blue of a tranquil evening sky. For a minute or so I remained watching the curate, and then I advanced, crouching and stepping with extreme care amid the broken crockery* that littered the floor.

3   I touched the curate's leg, and he started so violently that a mass of plaster went sliding down outside and fell with a loud impact. I gripped his arm, fearing he might cry out, and for a long time we crouched motionless. Then I turned to see how much of our rampart remained. The detachment of the plaster had left a vertical slit open in the debris, and by raising myself cautiously across a beam I was able to see out of this gap into what had been overnight a quiet suburban roadway. Vast, indeed, was the change that we beheld.

4 The fifth cylinder must have fallen right into the midst of the house we had first visited. The building had vanished, completely smashed, pulverised, and dispersed by the blow. The cylinder lay now far beneath the original foundations—deep in a hole, already vastly larger than the pit I had looked into at Woking. The earth all round it had splashed under that tremendous impact—"splashed" is the only word—and lay in heaped

piles that hid the masses of the adjacent houses. It had behaved exactly like mud under the violent blow of a hammer. Our house had collapsed backward; the front portion, even on the ground floor, had been destroyed completely; by a chance the kitchen and scullery had escaped, and stood buried now under soil and ruins, closed in by tons of earth on every side save towards the cylinder. Over that aspect we hung now on the very edge of the great circular pit the Martians were engaged in making. The heavy beating sound was evidently just behind us, and ever and again a bright green vapour drove up like a veil across our peephole.

5 The cylinder was already opened in the centre of the pit, and on the farther edge of the pit, amid the smashed and gravel-heaped shrubbery, one of the great fighting-machines, deserted by its occupant, stood stiff and tall against the evening sky.

---

*scullery – a small room near a kitchen

*curate – a clergyman in charge of a parish

*crockery – eating dishes

10 What style, or genre, of writing is this selection?

A. technical writing

B. science fiction

C. autobiography

D. myth

11 The point of view of this selection is

A. first person.

B. second person.

C. third person.

D. omniscient.

12 What is the tone of this excerpt?

A. humorous

B. ironic

C. angry

D. suspenseful

Read the sentence from paragraph 2 in the box below.

> Through the aperture in the wall I could see the top of a tree touched with gold and the warm blue of a tranquil evening sky.

13 In the context of the passage, what does the above sentence emphasize?

A. The people on Earth were uninterested.

B. The Earth had been peaceful before the Martians arrived.

C. The Earth was ready to defend itself against the Martians.

D. The narrator loves to admire nature.

14 According to the excerpt, the curate is

A. ill-tempered.

B. frightened.

C. good-natured.

D. misunderstood.

11

English poet Christina G. Rossetti (1830–1894) is considered one of the most prominent female poets of the Victorian era. She was known for her irregular rhymes and songlike verses. As you read this poem, think about whether you perceive the world differently when you are very happy.

Use information from the poem to answer the questions that follow.

A Birthday

1 My heart is like a singing bird
     Whose nest is in a water'd shoot;
  My heart is like an apple-tree
     Whose boughs are bent with thick-set fruit;
5 My heart is like a rainbow shell
     That paddles in a halcyon* sea;
  My heart is gladder than all these,
     Because my love is come to me.

     Raise me on a dais* of silk and down;
10   Hang it with vair* and purple dyes;
  Carve it in doves and pomegranates,
     And peacocks with a hundred eyes;
  Work it in gold and silver grapes,
     In leaves and silver fleurs-de-lys*;
15 Because the birthday of my life
     Is come, my love is come to me.

—Christina G. Rossetti

*halcyon – peaceful
*dais – a raised platform
*vair – the bluish-gray and white fur of a squirrel
*fleur-de-lys – a type of flower with three petals

15 Which figure of speech is primarily used in the first stanza?

A. onomatopoeia

B. simile

C. metaphor

D. pun

16 What is the theme of this poem?

A. birth

B. love

C. change

D. peace

17 Which word best describes the mood in the second stanza?

A. ecstatic

B. nostalgic

C. sarcastic

D. somber

18 In lines 3–4, the poet compares her heart to an apple tree. This comparison means that

A. her heart is tall and broad.

B. her heart is happier in summertime.

C. her heart pumps blood to her arms.

D. her heart is full and blooming.

Write your answer to open-response question 19 in the space provided in your Student Answer Booklet.

19 Explain why "A Birthday" is an appropriate title for Christina G. Rossetti's poem. Use relevant and specific information from this poem to support your answer.

English Language Arts
LANGUAGE AND LITERATURE: SESSION 2

DIRECTIONS

This session contains one reading selection with seven multiple-choice questions and one open-response question. Mark your answers to these questions in the spaces provided in your Student Answer Booklet (page 241).

Sometimes spending time with an old friend brings back memories of who we once were, as well as people we once knew. In this excerpt from the opening of My Ántonia *by Willa Cather, two friends reminisce about an extraordinary Bohemian girl, Ántonia, they knew a long time ago.*

Read the excerpt and answer the questions that follow.

from My Ántonia
by Willa Cather

1   Last summer I happened to be crossing the plains of Iowa in a season of intense heat, and it was my good fortune to have for a traveling companion James Quayle Burden—Jim Burden, as we still call him in the West. He and I are old friends—we grew up together in the same Nebraska town—and we had much to say to each other. While the train flashed through never-ending miles of ripe wheat, by country towns and bright-flowered pastures and oak groves wilting in the sun, we sat in the observation car, where the woodwork was hot to the touch and red dust lay deep over everything. The dust and heat, the burning wind, reminded us of many things. We were talking about what it is like to spend one's childhood in little towns like these, buried in wheat and corn, under stimulating extremes of climate: burning summers when the world lies green and billowy beneath a brilliant sky, when one is fairly stifled in vegetation, in the color and smell of strong weeds and heavy harvests; blustery winters with little snow, when the whole country is stripped bare and gray as sheet-iron. We agreed that no one who had not grown up in a little prairie town could know anything about it. It was a kind of freemasonry*, we said.

2   Although Jim Burden and I both live in New York, and are old friends, I do not see much of him there. He is legal counsel for one of the great Western railways, and is sometimes away from his New York office for weeks together. That is one reason why we do not often meet. Another is that I do not like his wife.

3   When Jim was still an obscure young lawyer, struggling to make his way in New York, his career was suddenly advanced by a

brilliant marriage. Genevieve Whitney was the only daughter of a distinguished man. Her marriage with young Burden was the subject of sharp comment at the time. It was said she had been brutally jilted by her cousin, Rutland Whitney, and that she married this unknown man from the West out of bravado. She was a restless, headstrong girl, even then, who liked to astonish her friends. Later, when I knew her, she was always doing something unexpected. She gave one of her town houses for a Suffrage headquarters, produced one of her own plays at the Princess Theater, was arrested for picketing during a garment-makers' strike, etc. I am never able to believe that she has much feeling for the causes to which she lends her name and her fleeting interest. She is handsome, energetic, executive, but to me she seems unimpressionable and temperamentally incapable of enthusiasm. Her husband's quiet tastes irritate her, I think, and she finds it worth while to play the patroness to a group of young poets and painters of advanced ideas and mediocre ability. She has her own fortune and lives her own life. For some reason, she wishes to remain Mrs. James Burden.

4   As for Jim, no disappointments have been severe enough to chill his naturally romantic and ardent disposition. This disposition, though it often made him seem very funny when he was a boy, has been one of the strongest elements in his success. He loves with a personal passion the great country through which his railway runs and branches. His faith in it and his knowledge of it have played an important part in its development. He is always able to raise capital for new enterprises in Wyoming or Montana, and has helped young men out there to do remarkable things in mines and timber and oil. If a young man with an idea can once get Jim Burden's attention, can manage to accompany him when he goes off into the wilds hunting for lost parks or exploring new canyons, then the money which means action is usually forthcoming. Jim is still able to lose himself in those big Western dreams. Though he is over forty now, he meets new people and new enterprises with the impulsiveness by which his boyhood friends remember him. He never seems to me to grow older. His fresh color and sandy hair and quick-changing blue eyes are those of a young man, and his sympathetic, solicitous interest in women is as youthful as it is Western and American.

5   During that burning day when we were crossing Iowa, our talk kept returning to a central figure, a Bohemian girl whom we had known long ago and whom both of us admired. More than any other person we

remembered, this girl seemed to mean to us the country, the conditions, the whole adventure of our childhood. To speak her name was to call up pictures of people and places, to set a quiet drama going in one's brain. I had lost sight of her altogether, but Jim had found her again after long years, had renewed a friendship that meant a great deal to him, and out of his busy life had set apart time enough to enjoy that friendship. His mind was full of her that day. He made me see her again, feel her presence, revived all my old affection for her.

6   "I can't see," he said impetuously, "why you have never written anything about Ántonia."

7   I told him I had always felt that other people—he himself, for one—knew her much better than I. I was ready, however, to make an agreement with him; I would set down on paper all that I remembered of Ántonia if he would do the same. We might, in this way, get a picture of her.

8   He rumpled his hair with a quick, excited gesture, which with him often announces a new determination, and I could see that my suggestion took hold of him. "Maybe I will, maybe I will!" he declared. He stared out of the window for a few moments, and when he turned to me again his eyes had the sudden clearness that comes from something the mind itself sees. "Of course," he said, "I should have to do it in a direct way, and say a great deal about myself. It's through myself that I knew and felt her, and I've had no practice in any other form of presentation."

9   I told him that how he knew her and felt her was exactly what I most wanted to know about Ántonia. He had had opportunities that I, as a little girl who watched her come and go, had not.

10   Months afterward Jim Burden arrived at my apartment one stormy winter afternoon, with a bulging legal portfolio sheltered under his fur overcoat. He brought it into the sitting-room with him and tapped it with some pride as he stood warming his hands.

11   "I finished it last night—the thing about Ántonia," he said. "Now, what about yours?"

12   I had to confess that mine had not gone beyond a few straggling notes.

13   "Notes? I didn't make any." He drank his tea all at once and put down the cup. "I didn't arrange or rearrange. I simply wrote down what of herself and myself and other people Ántonia's name recalls to me. I suppose it hasn't any form. It hasn't any title, either." He went into the next room, sat down at my desk and wrote on the pinkish face of the portfolio the word, "Ántonia." He frowned at this a moment, then prefixed another word, making it "My Ántonia." That seemed to satisfy him.

14   "Read it as soon as you can," he said, rising, "but don't let it influence your own story."

15   My own story was never written, but the following narrative is Jim's manuscript, substantially as he brought it to me.

----

*freemasonry – friendship and sympathy between a group of people

20 According to the excerpt, what is one reason the narrator seldom sees Jim Burden?

A. The narrator spends most of her time traveling.

B. Jim is frequently away from his New York office.

C. Jim's wife doesn't like the narrator.

D. The narrator's husband doesn't like Jim.

21 Which of the following **best** expresses the narrator's mood throughout the excerpt?

A. bitter about Jim's lifestyle

B. depressed to be traveling west again

C. nostalgic for the life she once knew

D. eager to write a novel about Ántonia

22 According to this excerpt, what is in the manuscript 'My Ántonia'?

A. the narrator's memories about Jim

B. "a few straggling notes"

C. the narrator's memories about Ántonia

D. Jim's memories about Ántonia

23 What does the author mean in the first paragraph when she describes the whole country as "gray as sheet-iron"?

A. The country looks shiny because it is bare.

B. The country looks dull because it is bare.

C. The country looks hard as if it were hard as steel.

D. The country is cold like the touch of steel.

24 In the excerpt, why was Jim Burden's manuscript described as "substantially as he brought it to me"?

A. It was well-crafted.

B. It was large and bulky.

C. It was read by many people.

D. It was emotional.

25 According to the excerpt, when the narrator remembered Ántonia, she also remembered

A. "the country, the conditions, the whole adventure of our childhood."

B. "the sudden clearness that comes from something the mind itself sees."

C. "The dust and the heat, the burning wind, reminded us of many things."

D. "the color and smell of strong weeds and heavy harvests."

26 The narrator says that she recalled small towns "buried in wheat and corn." This is an example of which figure of speech?

A. onomatopoeia

B. oxymoron

C. metaphor

D. hyperbole

Write your answer to open-response question 27 in the space provided in your Student Answer Booklet.

 27 Using information from the excerpt, what is the narrator's opinion of Jim Burden?

English Language Arts
LANGUAGE AND LITERATURE: SESSION 3

DIRECTIONS

**This session contains two reading selections with twelve multiple-choice questions
and one open-ended response question. Mark your answers to these questions in
the spaces provided in your Student Answer Booklet (page 242).**

*Dinosaurs have been extinct for millions of years, but other creatures from the time of the dinosaurs
are still alive. An example is the crocodile. To learn how this may have happened, the science
program* NOVA *interviewed Dr. James Perran Ross. Ross is a crocodile researcher for the Florida
Museum of Natural History and coordinator of the Crocodile Specialist Group.*

OUTLASTING THE DINOSAURS:

An Interview with Dr. James Perran Ross

1   **NOVA:** Why did crocodilians survive
when the dinosaurs went extinct?

2   **Ross:** The short answer is we don't know.
But we can look at what crocodiles do now
and how they work and speculate on some
things that may be involved. Crocodile
design has lasted an awfully long time. A
great many of the fossils of crocodiles are
virtually identical to the crocodiles we see
today. They seem to have successfully
adapted to their environment and have
undergone few changes. That's not
universally true, because crocodiles have
occasionally veered off into some other quite
interesting evolutionary lines. There is, for
instance, a secondary return to terrestrial life
among crocodiles. There's even a crocodile
that had hooves, and one speculates it must
have been a crocodile behaving like a small
deer or something.

3   **NOVA:** I've heard of a fossil croc in
Australia that was a tree-climber.

4   **Ross:** Conceivable. So they've periodically
left the mainstream, but all those little branches
didn't go anywhere. I think we have to look at
their basic design and concede that it's a good
way of being an amphibious predator. It really
works. I think one of the aspects that may play
to their survival is that they are extremely
tough and robust. We're learning now that the
immune systems of crocodiles, for instance,
are just incredible. They can sustain the most
frightful injuries. . . .

5   The adaptability of their behavior is also something that may play into their survival. It certainly has in modern times. We haven't lost a species of crocodile to extinction since humans have been dominant on the planet, even in the last few hundred years when our impact has been appalling. The reason appears to be in large part because crocodiles learn quickly and adapt to changes in their situation. They particularly learn to avoid dangerous situations very quickly. For research purposes, we find that we often have to change capture techniques, because it's very hard to catch them with the same trick twice.

6   **NOVA:** Would you call that intelligence?

7   **Ross:** Well, it's certainly rapid learning. Whether they sit and ponder or whether they just have neural synapses that fire quickly is a moot point. There are some people who keep crocodiles who claim that they are truly intelligent. I know some people whose opinions I respect who very sincerely believe that crocodiles know individual people and that they learn simple routines very readily, such as when the man with the bucket has food and when he doesn't.

8   They also become tame quite readily. There are alligator shows all over the country in which people routinely handle quite large alligators, which have become used to being handled and take it in their stride. There are a couple of well documented stories of truly tame crocodiles. The famous crocodile biologist Frederico Medem described a doctor who lived in Villavicencio, Colombia, who had a large *Crocodylus intermedius*, the Orinoco crocodile. He had raised it from a hatchling. It

was a female about 10 feet long, and it lived in his house. It played with his children, it played with the family dog. Villavicencio is up in the hills, and this crocodile liked to come into the house and lie in front of the fire on cool winter evenings. And it was housetrained.

9   **NOVA:** Never knew crocs could be so sociable.

10 **Ross:** They look a bit like logs, and everybody assumes they behave like logs. But studies have shown crocodilians to have quite complex social behavior. Individuals know other individuals and have long-term relationships with one another in terms of dominance and so forth. These relationships structure crocodile groups, certainly in captivity and probably also in the wild, in order to distribute access to food and even successful reproduction.

11 Of course, there's been some speculation that the dinosaurs also were more complex than we originally thought, in terms of things like maternal care. So again, I can't find any clear difference between what we know

crocodiles do and what we suspect dinosaurs might have done, which is why it's hard to answer the question, Why did crocs survive?

12   **NOVA:** Can you speculate on what else might have helped them outlast the dinosaurs?

13   **Ross:** Well, there is their association with water. Whatever devastated the terrestrial environments 65 million years ago—and the strong suspicion now is that it was an asteroid impact causing a long-term climatic change through dust in the atmosphere—appears to have had a less intense impact on freshwater environments. You can speculate on why crocodiles may have been able to survive that. For one thing, you can look at how crocodiles are kept in commercial captivity. In the less favorable situations, they're kept in complete darkness, under the most appalling conditions of bad hygiene. People fail to clean the water and toss them stinky dead stuff for food. Yet they go on thriving in these conditions. A nuclear-winter, meteor-impact scenario would be similar. It would be dark all the time—that apparently doesn't bother alligators. Dead stuff would be falling in the water as the rest of the fauna succumbed to the collapse of the food chain. The crocodiles conceivably were big enough to survive through that and under conditions that most other organisms couldn't tolerate.

14   **NOVA:** And crocs can go for long periods without eating, right?

15   **Ross:** Yes, they have an awesome capacity to deal with starvation. There are numerous examples of animals not feeding for an entire year.

28 The **main** purpose of this article is to

A. explain exactly why the dinosaurs became extinct.

B. describe the behavior and anatomy of crocodiles.

C. give reasons why crocodiles have survived so long.

D. give reasons why dinosaurs have survived so long.

29 According to Dr. Ross, crocodiles "look a bit like logs, and everybody assumes they behave like logs." Based on the information in this article, this comparison is

A. accurate.

B. not accurate.

C. a joke.

D. an insult.

30 In paragraph 2, the word *terrestrial* means

A. horrifying.

B. water-based.

C. land-based.

D. air-based.

Read the sentence from paragraph 5 in the box below.

> We haven't lost a species of crocodile to extinction since humans have been dominant on the planet, even in the last few hundred years when our impact has been appalling.

31 Which of the following statements expresses what Dr. Ross was saying?

A. He was emphasizing how much of a major force it took to make the dinosaurs extinct.

B. He was talking about the ways that humans endanger crocodiles.

C. He was emphasizing how many species of crocodiles exist today.

D. He was stressing the ability of crocodiles to survive.

32 In paragraph 8, Ross uses the example of the doctor from Villavicencio, Colombia, to show what idea about crocodiles?

A. There can be tame crocodiles.

B. Crocodiles in captivity need plenty of medical attention.

C. Crocodiles do not thrive in captivity.

D. There is a crocodile problem in Colombia.

33 In paragraph 7, what does the term *moot point* mean?

A. an issue that is debatable.

B. a question that is clearly explained.

C. a sharp edge that is dulled down by friction.

D. an issue that divides a community.

34 In paragraph 11, Dr. Ross says that "there's been some speculation that the dinosaurs also were more complex than we originally thought, in terms of things like maternal care." How does this speculation affect the mystery of why crocodiles outlived dinosaurs?

A. It answers many important questions.

B. It gives scientists a basis for comparison.

C. It solves the mystery completely.

D. It makes the mystery harder to solve.

Read the sentence from paragraph 3 in the box below:

> NOVA: I've heard of a fossil croc in Australia that was a tree-climber.

35 What is the *NOVA* interviewer attempting to accomplish with this statement?

A. The interviewer wants to hear more about mutated crocodiles.

B. The interviewer wanted to support Dr. Ross's statements.

C. The interviewer was testing Dr. Ross with a false statement.

D. The interviewer was keeping Dr. Ross from changing the subject.

Write your answer to open-response question 36 in the space provided in your Student Answer Booklet.

36 In the article, the author uses non-technical language and explanations to describe the adaptability and intelligence of the crocodile. Identify at least three such examples and explain how each one helps the reader understand crocodiles. Use relevant and specific information from the article to support your answer.

Tennessee Williams's The Glass Menagerie *is one of America's most well-known plays. In this scene, shy and sensitive Laura Wingfield is on her first date with a boy named Jim O'Connor. She is showing him her treasured collection of glass animals. Read this excerpt to learn how Jim helps Laura overcome her shyness.*

from The Glass Menagerie

by Tennessee Williams

1 **LAURA:**   Little articles of it, they're ornaments mostly! Most of them are little animals made out of glass, the tiniest little animals in the world. Mother calls them a glass menagerie*! Here's an example of one, if you'd like to see it! This one is one of the oldest. It's nearly thirteen. (*He*
5 *stretches out his hand.*) (*Music: "The Glass Menagerie."*) Oh, be careful—if you breathe, it breaks!
   JIM: I'd better not take it. I'm pretty clumsy with things.
   LAURA: Go on, I trust you with him! (*Places it in his palm.*) There now—you're holding him gently! Hold him over the light, he loves the
10 light! You see how the light shines through him?
   JIM: It sure docs shine!
   LAURA: I shouldn't be partial, but he is my favorite one.
   JIM: What kind of a thing is this one supposed to be?
   LAURA: Haven't you noticed the single horn on his forehead?
15 **JIM:**   A unicorn, huh?
   LAURA: Mmm-hmmm!
   JIM: Unicorns, aren't they extinct in the modern world?
   LAURA: I know!
   JIM: Poor little fellow, he must feel sort of lonesome.
20 **LAURA** (*smiling*).   Well, if he does he doesn't complain about it. He stays on a shelf with some horses that don't have horns and all of them seem to get along nicely together.

25

JIM: How do you know?

LAURA (*lightly*).   I haven't heard any arguments among them!

25   **JIM** (*grinning*).   No arguments, huh? Well, that's a pretty good sign! Where shall I set him?

LAURA: Put him on the table. They all like a change of scenery once in a while!

JIM (*stretching*).   Well, well, well, well—Look how big my shadow is
30   when I stretch!

LAURA: Oh, oh, yes—it stretches across the ceiling!

JIM (*crossing to door*).   I think it's stopped raining. (*Opens fire-escape door.*) Where does the music come from?

LAURA: From the Paradise Dance Hall across the alley.

35   **JIM:**   How about cutting the rug a little, Miss Wingfield?

LAURA: Oh, I—

JIM: Or is your program filled up? Let me have a look at it. (*Grasps imaginary card.*) Why, every dance is taken! I'll just have to scratch some out. (*Waltz Music: "La Golondrina."*) Ahhh, a waltz! (*He executes some*
40   *sweeping turns by himself then holds his arms toward Laura.*)

LAURA (*breathlessly*).   I—can't dance!

JIM: There you go, that inferiority stuff!

LAURA: I've never danced in my life!

JIM: Come on, try!

45   **LAURA:**   Oh, but I'd step on you!

JIM: I'm not made out of glass.

LAURA: How—how—how do we start?

JIM: Just leave it to me. You hold your arms out a little.

LAURA: Like this?

50   **JIM:**   A little bit higher. Right. Now don't tighten up, that's the main thing about it—relax.

LAURA (*laughs breathlessly*).   It's hard not to.

JIM: Okay.

LAURA: I'm afraid you can't budge me.

55   **JIM:**   What do you bet I can't? (*He swings her into motion.*)

LAURA: Goodness, yes, you can!

JIM: Let yourself go, now, Laura, just let yourself go.

LAURA: I'm—

JIM: Come on!

60   **LAURA:**   Trying!

JIM: Not so stiff—Easy does it!

LAURA: I know but I'm—

JIM: Loosen th' backbone! There now, that's a lot better.

LAURA: Am I?

65   **JIM:**   Lots, lots better! (*He moves her about the room in a clumsy waltz.*)

LAURA: Oh, my!

JIM: Ha-ha!

LAURA: Goodness, yes you can!

JIM: Ha-ha-ha! (*They suddenly bump into the table. Jim stops.*) What did we
70   hit on?
LAURA: Table.
JIM: Did something fall off it? I think—
LAURA: Yes.
JIM: I hope that it wasn't the little glass horse with the horn!
75 **LAURA:**   Yes.
JIM: Aw, aw, aw. Is it broken?
LAURA: Now it is just like all the other horses.
JIM: It's lost its—
LAURA: Horn! It doesn't matter. Maybe it's a blessing in disguise.
80 **JIM:**   You'll never forgive me. I bet that that was your favorite piece
    of glass.
LAURA: I don't have favorites much. It's no tragedy, Freckles. Glass
    breaks so easily. No matter how careful you are. The traffic jars the
    shelves and things fall off them.
85 **JIM:**   Still I'm awfully sorry that I was the cause.
LAURA (*smiling*).   I'll just imagine he had an operation.

---

*menagerie – an exhibition of wild animals, or the enclosure
 in which these animals are held

37 Which word best describes the interaction between Laura and Jim in this excerpt?

A. cordial

B. intense

C. complicated

D. aloof

38 According to the excerpt, why does Jim think the unicorn must be lonesome?

A. It has to stay at home with Laura.

B. Its horn is broken off in an accident.

C. It is different than the other horses.

D. It is kept on a shelf by itself.

39 The breaking of the unicorn's single horn seems to **symbolize**

A. that now the unicorn will look like the other horses.

B. that Laura is overcoming the shyness that has restricted her.

C. that Jim will be guilty for having broken the glass animal.

D. that Laura's mother will be upset with her for dancing.

Read the lines from the excerpt in the box below.

> **LAURA:** I'm—
> **JIM:** Come on!
> **LAURA:** Trying!
> **JIM:** Not so stiff—
> Easy does it!
> **LAURA:** I know but I'm—

40 What is the purpose of the dashes (—) used in the above lines?

A. to show that Laura and Jim are fighting

B. to show that Laura and Jim are trying to whisper

C. to show that Laura is trying to control how much she says

D. to show that Laura and Jim are dancing awkwardly

Lessons and Reviews

LESSON 1

Students will acquire and use correctly an advanced reading vocabulary of English words, identifying meanings through an understanding of word relationships.

WHAT THIS STANDARD MEANS

For this objective, you might be asked to determine the meaning of an unfamiliar word or a figurative phrase. A figurative phrase has a meaning that is not literal. The sentence, "When I try to write, my mind is often blank" contains a figurative phrase. The sentence really means, "When I try to write, I can't think of what to say."

You can figure out the meaning of an unfamiliar word or figurative phrase by looking at the context, or the words and sentences around it.

STEP ONE **TEN-MINUTE LESSON**

Sample Passage

from Inside Mexico: A Peasant's Life

by Ian Campbell

1   QUERETARO, MEXICO—Early one hot afternoon I found myself outside the front door of the house and talking to one of the gardeners, a seventy-year-old man who finds odd jobs to do in the gated community where I live.

2   I know him fairly well. He has never quite been the same since he fell from a tree eighteen months ago. When he had failed to appear for some weeks I learned about his accident and got directions to his home. I found him shuffling about, not the strong and healthy man he had been previously, despite his good age. After a number of visits he agreed to come to see my doctor. But it was late to go. His broken forearm had set itself badly. And as for his injured back, an injection and pain-killers from the doctor helped but he refused to go for the X-rays the doctor recommended even though I offered to take him to the hospital and pay.

3   Ever since then, ask him how he is and he tends to rub his back and mention some pains but say with a broad smile *"Ay vamos!"*, which might be translated as "Now I'm OK." He is on his feet, able to work. "You have to expect something in life," he says. At least from his "something" he has survived. That he can work is all that matters to him. He can put up with a little pain.

4   On the hot afternoon I offered him a drink and he came inside and we began to talk.

5   I asked him when he had begun to work and he said when he was about eight years old. He worked with his step-father in the fields. He had no memory of his own father, who had died. With neither the step-father nor step-brothers were his relations good. Now, though the step-brothers live nearby, he has no contact with them. "Bad people," he says.

Sample Questions

 1 In paragraph 2, when the author said that the gardener was usually strong and healthy "despite his good age," the author meant that the gardener

A. lived an easy and relaxed life.

B. was a strong and healthy young man.

C. never revealed his true age to the author.

D. was strong and healthy even though he was old.

This question asks you to determine the meaning of the figurative phrase "despite his good age." Remember that a figurative phrase is not literal. The author does not mean that a certain age is actually better than another. Also remember to look for the best answer to the question. Don't choose the first answer that seems correct.

Answer choice A: Does the term "good age" refer to an easy and relaxed life? The author says that the gardener was normally strong and healthy, but the narrator also explains that the gardener's life had been difficult. His life had not been easy or relaxed, so this is probably not the correct choice.

Answer choice B: What does the author tell us about the gardener? He says that the gardener was strong and healthy. However, he does not say that the gardener was a young man; in fact, he says the gardener was seventy years old. This answer choice is incorrect.

Answer choice C: When the author writes "despite his good age," does he mean that the gardener never told how old he was? Think back to the information the author gives you about the gardener. Early in the selection the author says that the gardener was seventy years old. Since the author *does* know how old the gardener is, this answer choice is probably not the best one.

Answer choice D: This answer choice agrees that the gardener was strong and healthy, but substitutes the phrase "despite his good age" with "even though he was old." Do these phrases have the same meaning? The author told us that the gardener was seventy years old, which most people would consider old. Also, "despite" is the same as "even though." This is the best answer choice.

 **2** The word *relations* in paragraph 5 means

A. the members of a family.

B. knowledge of where other people live.

C. dealings with other people.

D. understanding of different beliefs.

Ⓐ   Ⓑ   Ⓒ   Ⓓ

You don't need to know the meaning of the word *relations* to answer this question. However, you have to look carefully at the words in paragraph 5 to determine its meaning. The paragraph tells us that the gardener did not have good relations with his step-father or step-brothers. He had "no contact with them" and thought they were "bad people." In deciding what *relations* means here, remember that many words have more than one meaning. Be very careful to read all your choices before making a decision.

Answer choice A: This answer choice says that *relations* is used to mean the members of a family. You may know that this is one of the meanings of the word *relations*. However, the question is whether this is the meaning used in paragraph 5. That paragraph talks about members of his family, but the word does not seem to refer to them. There is probably a better choice.

Answer choice B: Would not having good relations with someone be caused by not knowing where he or she lives? Paragraph 5 talks about how the gardener felt about his step-father and step-brothers, but he says that he knew the step-brothers lived nearby. He knew where they lived, so this is probably not the correct answer.

Answer choice C: Do relations with a person mean the way that you deal with him or her? This is one meaning of the word *relations*. Decide if this meaning fits the ideas in the paragraph. The paragraph talks about what the gardener thought about his family and how he dealt with them. This answer choice is probably the best, but you should read the last choice just to make sure.

Answer choice D: When the author says *relations*, does he mean understanding of different beliefs? The gardener may not have understood the beliefs of his stepfather and step-brothers, but the word *relations* means more than just that. This is not the best choice. Choice C is the correct answer.

3 In paragraph 1, when the author said that the man found "odd jobs" to do in his gated community, he meant that these jobs

A. paid little.

B. were small.

C. were strange.

D. seemed common.

Ⓐ   Ⓑ   Ⓒ   Ⓓ

Answer choice A: The man was a retired gardener, so we know that he did not work full time. He probably helped with small tasks that didn't take a long time. While he probably wasn't paid a great deal for these jobs, we don't know for sure how much he was paid, so this probably isn't the best answer choice.

Answer choice B: Odd jobs are most likely small jobs, since they can be done by a retired gardener. This is probably the best answer choice, but be sure to consider each answer option before making a decision.

Answer choice C: The word *odd* does mean "strange," but not in this instance. There is no indication that the jobs the gardener completed were strange, so this is not the best answer choice.

Answer choice D: Odd jobs are usually not common jobs. They are small jobs that require only a little work. Answer choice B is the correct answer.

STEP TWO SIDEBAR INSTRUCTION

Read the selection and answer the questions that follow. Use the *Sidebar Instruction* to help you choose the correct answer.

from China's Age of Invention

from the NOVA Website

1   The Rainbow Bridge built in the NOVA program "China Bridge" is just one of many important inventions that appeared during China's impressive Song Dynasty (A.D. 960-1280). This vibrant period in Chinese history was marked by economic prosperity and remarkable technological innovation. Read on to find out what China expert Robin D. S. Yates, Professor of History and East Asian Studies at McGill University in Montreal, Quebec, Canada, has to say about this exceptional era—and how it influenced the course of world history.

2   **NOVA:** Let's begin by providing a worldwide context for the Song Dynasty. In 1271, the Italian merchant Marco Polo is believed to have visited China. What was his impression of this very different world?

3   **Yates:** Well, there's a debate as to whether Marco Polo ever did, in fact, visit China. However, assuming Polo's account is real, what comes across most obviously is that he was utterly astonished at the size of the cities and the extent of commercial activity in China. The number of ships on Chinese canals and rivers far exceeded what Polo was familiar with in the cities of Italy, such as Venice or Genoa.

4   The Chinese had a very cultured and civilized society. Song Dynasty silks, for example, were remarkably advanced. The Chinese were using very sophisticated looms with up to 1,800 moving parts. China was simply far more developed technologically and culturally than any state in the West.

5   But one wonders whether Polo had actually visited, because of the things that he doesn't write about at all. He doesn't mention paper money and the bank note, which were both invented during the Song Dynasty. You would have thought that if he'd lived there for 20 years, he might have noticed it, because Western Europe didn't have it.

6   **NOVA:** What are some of the things that made these large, bustling Chinese cities unique in their time?

7   **Yates:** There is a strong connection between the increasing urbanization and the burgeoning commercialization of Chinese culture at this time. Merchants traveled from

36

one place to another, and a new group of scholar-officials was appointed to administer the country. The traveling merchants and officials wanted to eat the cuisine that they were used to in their local region. And people with some extra wealth in the urban centers also wanted to try food from different regions. So what developed was a new urban type of culture that included eating out in restaurants and the drinking of tea.

8   It was really in the Song Dynasty that tea reached its cult status. It was drunk out of very beautiful, extraordinarily exquisite tea bowls made from porcelain, one of the glories of the Song Dynasty. The word "china" is appropriate for porcelain, because the Chinese developed the technology for its production. The Song Dynasty ceramic industry was basically the first commercialized industry. They produced the pieces in mass quantities for the imperial palace, but also for this newly arisen class of scholar-officials and an urban elite and for these restaurants. Eventually, two of the main products the West wanted in the 17th, 18th, and 19th centuries were porcelain and tea, so much of the trade between East and West was based on those items.

9   With restaurants, common folk could eat out very, very cheaply on food such as fried noodles, which, it is said, Marco Polo introduced to the West. Although there's a lot of debate about that, the idea of spaghetti probably comes from China at about the time of the Song, possibly carried across the ocean by Arab traders, who are known to have established themselves in ports such as Canton by the ninth century.

10 **NOVA:** Tea and restaurants are certainly two important gifts the Song people gave to the world. What were some of the other Chinese inventions of this period that had a profound influence on the course of civilization?

11 **Yates:** Gunpowder completely transformed the way wars were waged and contributed to the eventual establishment of might over right. In my own research, I have been able to refute the common notion that the Chinese invented gunpowder but only used it for fireworks. I'm sure that they discovered military uses for it. I have found the earliest illustration of a cannon in the world, which dates from the change-over from the Northern Song to the Southern Song around 1127, which was 150 years before the development of the cannon in the West. The Song also used gunpowder to make fire lances—actually flame throwers—and many other gunpowder weapons, such as anti-personnel mines, which are thankfully now being taken out of general use.

1 Which word or phrase from paragraph 7 helps the reader understand the meaning of the word *burgeoning*?

A. strong connection

B. increasing

C. Chinese culture

D. between

Ⓐ Ⓑ Ⓒ Ⓓ

SIDEBAR INSTRUCTION

Find the word *burgeoning* in the paragraph. Then read the entire sentence. To what is *burgeoning* compared? Which word or words in the answer choices helps you figure out the meaning of *burgeoning*?

2 What does the word *context* mean in paragraph 2?

A. overview

B. prediction

C. building

D. debate

Ⓐ Ⓑ Ⓒ Ⓓ

SIDEBAR INSTRUCTION

Find the word *context* in paragraph 2. What does it say about the first thing the interviewer wants to discuss? What word helps you understand the meaning of *context*?

3 In paragraph 11, what does the phrase "might over right" mean?

A. people disagreeing about what is right

B. many countries being in conflict

C. weaker people being protected

D. stronger people making the rules

Ⓐ Ⓑ Ⓒ Ⓓ

SIDEBAR INSTRUCTION

Read the first sentence of paragraph 11. What did the invention of gunpowder do to the way people behaved? How would that have caused "might over right"?

4 What does the word *innovation* mean in paragraph 1?

A. imaginative

B. progress

C. international trade

D. obsession

Ⓐ Ⓑ Ⓒ Ⓓ

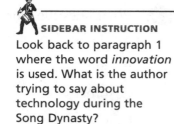

SIDEBAR INSTRUCTION
Look back to paragraph 1 where the word *innovation* is used. What is the author trying to say about technology during the Song Dynasty?

5 In paragraph 4, what does the word *sophisticated* mean?

A. highly advanced

B. overly complicated

C. confusing

D. fast-moving

Ⓐ Ⓑ Ⓒ Ⓓ

SIDEBAR INSTRUCTION
Refer back to the sentence in paragraph 4 in which *sophisticated* is used. What point is the author trying to make in that sentence?

6 Which word from paragraph 8 helps the reader understand the meaning of the word *exquisite*?

A. status

B. appropriate

C. beautiful

D. porcelain

Ⓐ Ⓑ Ⓒ Ⓓ

SIDEBAR INSTRUCTION
Go back and reread paragraph 8. What are the tea bowls like? Which word helps you understand that they are very nice?

7 What does the word *administer* mean in paragraph 7?

A. direct

B. give

C. process

D. dispense

Ⓐ Ⓑ Ⓒ Ⓓ

SIDEBAR INSTRUCTION
Go back and reread paragraph 7. The word *administer* is used in an uncommon way. Choose the answer choice that is closest in meaning to the way *administer* is used in the paragraph.

8 In paragraph 11, what does *refute* mean?

A. support

B. prove false

C. comprehend

D. communicate

Ⓐ Ⓑ Ⓒ Ⓓ

SIDEBAR INSTRUCTION
Carefully read the entire paragraph. What is the author saying about the common notion that the Chinese invented gunpowder but only used it for fireworks?

9 What commodities and "sophisticated innovations" did the Chinese successfully commercialize during the Song Dynasty? Be specific and give reasons why Western travelers were impressed with these inventions.

_____

_____

_____

_____

_____

_____

_____

Read the selection. Then answer the questions that follow.

from **The Airmail Bowling Ball**

by Anne Tyler

1   On Waverly Street, everybody knew everybody else. It was only one short block, after all—a narrow strip of patched and repatched pavement, bracketed between a high stone cemetery wall at one end and the commercial clutter of Govans Road at the other. The trees were elderly maples with lumpy, bulbous trunks. The squat clapboard houses seemed mostly front porch.

2   And each house had its own particular role to play. Number Nine, for instance, was foreign. A constantly shifting assortment of Middle Eastern graduate students came and went, attended classes at Johns Hopkins, and the scent of exotic spices drifted from their kitchen every evening at suppertime. Number Six was referred to as the newlyweds', although the Crains had been married two years now and were beginning to look a bit worn around the edges. And Number Eight was the Bedloe family. They were never just the Bedloes, but the Bedloe *family*, Waverly Street's version of the ideal, apple-pie household; two amiable parents, three good-looking children, a dog, a cat, a scattering of goldfish.

3   In fact, the oldest of those children had long ago married and left—moved out to Baltimore County and started a family of her own—and the second-born was nearing thirty. But somehow the Bedloes were stuck in people's minds at a stage from a dozen years back, when Claudia was a college girl in bobby socks and Danny was captain of his high-school football team and Ian, the baby (his parents' big surprise), was still tearing down the sidewalk on his tricycle with a miniature license plate from a cereal box wired to the handlebar.

4   Now Ian was seventeen and, like the rest of his family, large-boned and handsome and easygoing, quick to make friends, fond of a good time. He had the Bedloe golden-brown hair, golden skin, and sleepy-looking brown eyes, although his mouth was his mother's, a pale beige mouth quirking upward at the corners. He liked to wear ragged jeans and plaid shirts—cotton broadcloth in summer, flannel in winter—unbuttoned all the way to expose a stretched-out T-shirt underneath. His shoes were high-top sneakers held together with electrical tape. This was in 1965, when Poe High School still maintained at least a vestige of dress code, and his teachers were forever sending him home to put on something more presentable. (But his mother was likely to greet him in baggy, lint-covered slacks and one of his own shirts, her fading blond curls pinned scrappily back with a granddaughter's pink plastic hairbow. She would not have passed the dress code either.) Also, there were complaints about the quality of Ian's schoolwork. He was bright, his teachers said, but lazy. Content to slide through with low B's or even C's. It was the spring of his junior year and if he didn't soon

mend his ways, no self-respecting college would have him.

5   Ian listened to all this with a tolerant, bemused expression. Things would turn out fine, he felt. Hadn't they always? (None of the Bedloes was a worrier.) Crowds of loyal friends had surrounded him since kindergarten. His sweetheart, Cicely Brown, was the prettiest girl in the junior class. His mother doted on him and his father—Poe's combination algebra teacher and baseball coach—let him pitch in nearly every game, and not just because they were related, either. His father claimed Ian had talent. In fact sometimes Ian daydreamed about pitching for the Orioles, but he knew he didn't have that much talent. He was a medium kind of guy, all in all.

6   Even so, there were moments when he believed that someday, somehow, he was going to end up famous. Famous for what, he couldn't quite say; but he'd be walking up the back steps or something and all at once he would imagine a camera zooming in on him, filming his life story. He imagined the level, cultured voice of his biographer saying, "Ian climbed the steps. He opened the door. He entered the kitchen."

7   "Have a good day, hon?" his mother asked passing through with a laundry basket.

8   "Oh," he said, "the usual run of scholastic triumphs and athletic glories." And he set his books on the table.

10 What does the word *doted* mean in paragraph 5?

A. depended on

B. gossiped about

C. fussed over

D. helped out

Ⓐ Ⓑ Ⓒ Ⓓ

11 In paragraph 2, the word *family* is emphasized in order to give the reader what idea?

A. the sarcasm of the author

B. the bitterness of the neighbors

C. the wholesomeness of the Bedloe family

D. the number of Bedloe family members

Ⓐ Ⓑ Ⓒ Ⓓ

12 In paragraph 4, what is the word *vestige* used to mean?

A. a small remaining amount

B. a false hope few people share

C. an illusion made to deceive

D. an old-fashioned memory

Ⓐ Ⓑ Ⓒ Ⓓ

13 Which word from paragraph 2 helps the reader understand the meaning of the word *exotic*?

A. particular

B. scent

C. shifting

D. foreign

Ⓐ Ⓑ Ⓒ Ⓓ

14 What does the word *bulbous* mean in paragraph 1?

A. brownish

B. roundish

C. squarish

D. cracked

Ⓐ Ⓑ Ⓒ Ⓓ

15 In paragraph 2, what does the phrase "worn around the edges" mean?

A. old

B. irritated

C. overweight

D. puzzled

Ⓐ Ⓑ Ⓒ Ⓓ

16 What does the word *quirking* mean in paragraph 4?

A. wrinkling

B. smiling

C. curving

D. smoothing

Ⓐ Ⓑ Ⓒ Ⓓ

17 In paragraph 2, what is the word *scattering* used to mean?

A. small bunch

B. huge collection

C. great variety

D. large quantity

Ⓐ Ⓑ Ⓒ Ⓓ

18 What does Ian mean in the last sentence of the passage when he says that his day consisted of "the usual run of scholastic triumphs and athletic glories"? Use details and information from the passage to support your answer.

_____

_____

_____

_____

_____

_____

_____

_____

_____

_____

LESSON 2

Students will identify, describe, and apply knowledge of the structure and origins of the English language and standard English conventions for sentence structure, usage, punctuation, capitalization, and spelling.

WHAT THIS STANDARD MEANS

For this objective, you will be asked to closely examine what you read in order to learn more about the topic, the author, and the language. You will be asked to look closely at an author's sentences. Sentences are much more than just groups of words. They come in many varieties, including simple, compound, complex, and compound-complex. Sentences can also have special features, such as ellipses and dashes, which affect the flow and meaning of the sentence. Deciding why the author structured a sentence in a particular way can help you understand what you are reading.

The words in a sentence can also reveal more information. There are many kinds of words and phrases, including participles, gerunds, and infinitives. These can be used in many ways to enhance the meaning of a sentence. Additionally, every word has an origin, or a time and place in which it was created. Determining the origin of a word can help you understand its meaning. In this lesson, you will be asked to make decisions about why authors choose certain words and how they build their sentences.

STEP ONE | TEN-MINUTE LESSON

Sample Passage

Read the poems. Then answer the questions that follow.

Design

by Robert Frost

I found a dimpled spider, fat and white,
On a white heal-all, holding up a moth
Like a white piece of rigid satin cloth—
Assorted characters of death and blight
5   Mixed ready to begin the morning right,
Like the ingredients of a witches' broth—
A snow-drop spider, a flower like a froth,
And dead wings carried like a paper kite.

What had that flower to do with being white,
10   The wayside blue and innocent heal-all?
What brought the kindred spider to that height,
Then steered the white moth thither in the night?
What but design of darkness to appall?—
If design govern in a thing so small.

Neither Out Far Nor In Deep

By Robert Frost

The people along the sand
All turn and look one way.
They turn their back on the land.
They look at the sea all day.

5   As long as it takes to pass
A ship keeps raising its hull;
The wetter ground like glass
Reflects a standing gull.

The land may vary more;
10 But wherever the truth may be—
The water comes ashore,
And the people look at the sea.

They cannot look out far.
They cannot look in deep.
15 But when was that ever a bar
To any watch they keep?

Sample Questions

Read the lines from "Design" in the box below.

> Assorted characters of death and blight
> Mixed ready to begin the morning right,
> Like the incredients of a witches' broth—
> A snow-drop spider, a flower like a froth,
> And dead wings carried like a paper kite.

1 The author uses a dash at the end of the third line to

A. indicate that the reader should read more slowly.

B. separate an idea from a description of that idea.

C. show that the spiders and moths are hesitating.

D introduce entirely new ideas into the poem.

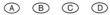

This question asks you to determine why the author uses a dash in this excerpt. Read the lines carefully. What is the author talking about? What purpose does the dash serve here?

Answer choice A: Dashes are not used to indicate slowness. Also, the ideas in the excerpt here don't need to be read any more slowly or quickly than the rest of the poem. This choice is not the best answer.

Answer choice B: In the excerpt, the author talks about "the ingredients of a witches' broth" and then uses the dash. After the dash, he lists the spider, the flower, and the moth's wings. These three things are the witches' ingredients. The dash appears to separate an idea from its description. This is probably the correct answer choice. However, be sure to consider each answer choice before making a selection.

Answer choice C: The author's main point in writing this poem is to show that the events that take place happen naturally and without hesitation. The creatures he mentions do not hesitate. The dash is probably not meant to show that. This answer choice is not the correct one.

Answer choice D: Dashes can be used to bring new ideas into a piece of writing. However, in this case, the ideas that are linked by the dash (the spider, the flower, and the moth's wings) have already been discussed earlier in the poem. They are not entirely new ideas. Choice B is the best answer.

Read the lines from "Neither Out Far Nor In Deep" in the box below.

> They cannot look out far.
> They cannot look in deep.

2 Which of the following writing techniques do these sentences illustrate?

A. exaggeration

B. simile

C. parallel structure

D. sensory imagery

Ⓐ   Ⓑ   Ⓒ   Ⓓ

This question asks you to identify the writing technique the author is using in the lines from the poem shown in the box. Read these lines several times. Think about how they are different from regular English usage.

Answer choice A: An author can use exaggeration to emphasize a point or interest a reader. However, the ideas in these lines from the poem do not seem exaggerated. They seem to be completely literal. This choice is probably not the best answer.

Answer choice B: A simile compares two seemingly unlike things using terms such as *like* or *as*. Nothing is being compared in these lines from the poem. Therefore, this is not the correct answer.

Answer choice C: When authors use parallel structure, they repeat their sentence structure. These two sentences are very similar in structure. The author clearly did this on purpose to emphasize his point. This is probably the best choice, but read on to make sure.

Answer choice D: While the author does refer to people looking, he doesn't elaborate on the sense of sight or any other senses or imagery. This is not the best answer. Choice C is the best answer.

Read these lines from "Neither Out Far Nor In Deep" in the box below.

> The wetter ground like glass.
> Reflects a standing gull.

3 In the sentence above, the word *wetter* is used as

A. a conjunction.

B. a verb.

C. a preposition.

D. an adjective.

Answer choice A: A conjunction serves to connect other words. Examples of conjunctions are *and*, *as*, and *but*. In this sentence, *wetter* does not connect any words. This is not the correct answer choice.

Answer choice B: A verb indicates action. In this sentence, the word *reflects* is a verb. *Wetter* does not involve any action. It is not a verb. Therefore, this is not the correct answer.

Answer choice C: A preposition is a word or phrase that links nouns and phrases to other parts of the sentence. Examples of prepositions are *during*, *over*, and *beside*. In this excerpt, *wetter* does not link nouns or phrases with anything. This is not the right answer choice.

Answer choice D: An adjective is a word that modifies or describes a noun. In this case, *wetter* is a descriptive word that modifies *ground*. It tells us that the ground is very wet. This word is an adjective. Answer choice D is the best choice.

STEP TWO SIDEBAR INSTRUCTION

Read the selection and answer the questions that follow. Use the Sidebar Instruction to help you choose the correct answer.

THE HOUSE ON MANGO STREET

by Sandra Cisneros

1   We didn't always live on Mango Street. Before that we lived on Loomis on the third floor, and before that we lived on Keeler. Before Keeler it was Paulina, and before that I can't remember. But what I remember most is moving a lot. Each time it seemed there'd be one more of us. By the time we got to Mango Street we were six—Mama, Papa, Carlos, Kiki, my sister Nenny, and me.

2   The house on Mango Street is ours, and we don't have to pay rent to anybody, or share the yard with the people downstairs, or be careful not to make too much noise, and there isn't a landlord banging on the ceiling with a broom. But even so, it's not the house we'd thought we'd get.

3   We had to leave the flat on Loomis quick. The water pipes broke and the landlord wouldn't fix them because the house was too old. We had to leave fast. We were using the washroom next door and carrying water over in empty milk gallons. That's why Mama and Papa looked for a house, and that's why we moved into the house on Mango Street, far away, on the other side of town.

4   They always told us that one day we would move into a house, a real house that would be ours for always so we wouldn't have to move each year. And our house would have running water and pipes that worked. And inside it would have real stairs, not hallway stairs, but stairs inside like the houses on T.V. And we'd have a basement and at least three washrooms so when we took a bath we wouldn't have to tell everybody. Our house would be white with trees around it, a great big yard and grass growing without a fence. This was the house Papa talked about when he held a lottery ticket and this was the house Mama dreamed up in the stories she told us before we went to bed.

5   But the house on Mango Street is not the way they told it at all. It's small and red with tight steps in front and windows so small you'd think they were holding their breath. Bricks are crumbling in places, and the front door is so swollen you have to push hard to get in. There is no front yard, only four little elms the city planted by the curb. Out back is a small garage for the car we don't own yet and a small yard that looks smaller between the two buildings on either side. There are stairs in our house, but they're ordinary hallway stairs, and the house has only one washroom. Everybody has to share a bedroom—Mama and Papa, Carlos and Kiki, me and Nenny.

6   Once when we were living on Loomis, a nun from my school passed by and saw me playing out front. The laundromat downstairs had been boarded up because it had been robbed two days before and the owner had painted on the wood YES WE'RE OPEN so as not to lose business.

7   Where do you live? she asked.

8   There, I said pointing up to the third floor.

9   You live *there?*

10   *There.* I had to look to where she pointed—the third floor, the paint peeling, wooden bars Papa had nailed on the windows so we wouldn't fall out. You live *there?* The way she said it made me feel like nothing. *There.* I lived *there.* I nodded.

11   I knew then I had to have a house. A real house. One I could point to. But this isn't it. The house on Mango Street isn't it. For the time being, Mama says. Temporary, says Papa. But I know how those things go.

Read the sentence from the selection in the box below.

> Bricks are crumbling in places, and the front door is so swollen you have to push hard to get in.

1 The line above is an example of a

A. simple sentence.

B. compound sentence.

C. complex sentence.

D. compound-complex sentence.

Ⓐ Ⓑ Ⓒ Ⓓ

SIDEBAR INSTRUCTION
Think about what you know of these answer choices. Then read the sentence carefully. What are the parts of the sentence?

2 What is the purpose of the italics in paragraph 10?

A. to show that the speaker likes where she lives

B. to prepare the reader for details about her home

C. to emphasize that her home is not nice

D. to imply that her home is hard to find

Ⓐ Ⓑ Ⓒ Ⓓ

SIDEBAR INSTRUCTION
Think about what the speaker says about her house. Why is the nun surprised to know where she lives?

Read the lines from the selection in the box below.

> I knew then I had to have a house. A real
> house. One I could point to.

3 Why does the author use two sentence fragments?

A. to prepare the reader for a change in thought

B. to emphasize the importance of having a house

C. to show that the narrator has lived in many different houses

D. to imply that the narrator is having trouble gathering her thoughts

Ⓐ Ⓑ Ⓒ Ⓓ

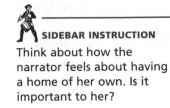

SIDEBAR INSTRUCTION
Think about how the narrator feels about having a home of her own. Is it important to her?

This is a dictionary entry for the word *nun*.

nun (ńən) n. [ME. fr OE nunne, fr LL nonna]: a woman belonging to a religious order; esp: one under solemn vows of poverty, chastity, and obedience.

4 According to the entry, from which language did the word *nun* originate?

A. Late Latin

B. Old English

C. French

D. Middle English

Ⓐ Ⓑ Ⓒ Ⓓ

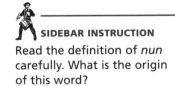

SIDEBAR INSTRUCTION
Read the definition of *nun* carefully. What is the origin of this word?

Read these lines from the passage in the box below.

> We had to leave the flat on Loomis quick.
> The water pipes broke and the landlord
> wouldn't fix them because the house was
> too old. We had to leave fast.

5 The author repeats the same idea here to

   A. illustrate the condition of the house.

   B. foreshadow an upcoming change.

   C. emphasize the urgency of the situation.

   D. create a mood of suspense and mystery.

ⓐ ⓑ ⓒ ⓓ

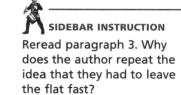

SIDEBAR INSTRUCTION
Reread paragraph 3. Why
does the author repeat the
idea that they had to leave
the flat fast?

6 The author uses images to describe her house on Mango Street.
Using relevant and specific details, describe her house.

_____

_____

_____

_____

_____

_____

_____

_____

_____

STEP THREE ON YOUR OWN

Read the following selection and answer the questions.

from A Tale of Two Cities

by Charles Dickens

1   It was the best of times, it was the worst of times, it was the age of wisdom, it was the age of foolishness, it was the epoch of belief, it was the epoch of incredulity, it was the season of Light, it was the season of Darkness, it was the spring of hope, it was the winter of despair, we had everything before us, we had nothing before us, we were all going direct to Heaven, we were all going direct the other way—in short, the period was so far like the present period, that some of its noisiest authorities insisted on its being received, for good or for evil, in the superlative degree of comparison only.

2   There were a king with a large jaw and a queen with a plain face, on the throne of England; there were a king with a large jaw and a queen with a fair face, on the throne of France. In both countries it was clearer than crystal to the lords of the State preserves of loaves and fishes, that things in general were settled for ever.

3   It was the year of Our Lord one thousand seven hundred and seventy-five. Spiritual revelations were conceded to England at that favoured period, as at this. Mrs. Southcott had recently attained her five-and-twentieth blessed birthday, of whom a prophetic* private in the Life Guards had heralded the sublime* appearance by announcing that arrangements were made for the swallowing up of London and Westminster. . . . Mere messages in the earthly order of events had lately come to the English Crown and People from a Congress of British subjects in America; which, strange to relate, have proved more important to the human race than any communications yet received through any of the chickens of the Cock-lane brood.

4   France, less favoured on the whole as to matters spiritual than her sister of the shield and trident, rolled with exceeding smoothness down the hill, making paper money and spending it. Under the guidance of her Christian pastors, she entertained herself, besides, with such humane achievements as sentencing a youth to have his hands cut off, his tongue torn out with pincers*, and his

body burned alive, because he had not kneeled down in the rain to do honour to a dirty procession of monks which passed within his view, at a distance of some fifty or sixty yards. It is likely enough that, rooted in the woods of France and Norway, there were growing trees, when that sufferer was put to death, already marked by the woodman, Fate, to come down to be sawn into boards, to make a certain moveable framework with a sack and a knife in it, terrible in history. It is likely enough that in the rough outhouses of some tillers of the heavy lands adjacent to Paris, there were sheltered from the weather that very day, rude carts, bespattered with rustic mire, snuffed about by pigs, and roosted in by poultry, which the Farmer, Death, had already set apart to be his tumbrels of the Revolution. But that Woodman and that Farmer, though they work unceasingly, work silently, and no one heard them as they went about with muffled tread: the rather, forasmuch as to entertain any suspicion that they were awake, was to be atheistical and traitorous.

5 In England, there was scarcely an amount of order and protection to justify much national boasting. Daring burglaries by armed men, and highway robberies, took place in the capital itself every night; families were publicly cautioned not to go out of town without removing their furniture to upholsterers' warehouses for security; the highwayman* in the dark was a City tradesman in the light, and, being recognized and challenged by his fellow-tradesman whom he stopped in his character of "the Captain," gallantly shot him through the head and rode away; the mail was waylaid by seven robbers, and the guard shot three dead, and then got shot dead himself by the other four, "in consequence of the failure of his ammunition;" after which the mail was robbed in peace; that magnificent potentate, the Lord Mayor of London, was made to stand and deliver on Turnham Green, by one highwayman, who despoiled* the illustrious creature in sight of all his retinue*; prisoners

in London gaols fought battles with their turnkeys, and the majesty of the law fired blunderbusses* in among them, loaded with rounds of shot and ball; thieves snipped off diamond crosses from the necks of noble lords at Court drawing-rooms; musketeers went into St. Gile's, to search for contraband goods, and the mob fired on the musketeers, and the musketeers fired on the mob; and nobody thought any of these occurrences much out of the common way. In the midst of them, the hangman, ever busy and ever worse than useless, was in constant requisition; now, stringing up long rows of miscellaneous criminals; now, hanging a housebreaker on Saturday who had been taken on Tuesday; now, burning people in the hand at Newgate by the dozen, and now burning pamphlets at the door of Westminster Hall; to-day, taking the life of an atrocious murderer, and to-morrow of a wretched pilferer who had robbed a farmer's boy of sixpence.

6 All these things, and a thousand like them, came to pass in and close upon the dear old year one thousand seven hundred and seventy-five. Environed by them, while the Woodman and the Farmer worked unheeded, those two of the large jaws, and those other two of the plain and the fair faces, trod with stir enough, and carried their divine rights with a high hand. Thus did the year one thousand seven hundred and seventy-five conduct their Greatnesses, and myriads* of small creatures—the creatures of this chronicle among the rest—along the roads that lay before them.

---

* *prophetic* — foretelling events

* *sublime* — lofty and grand in thought, expression and manner

* *pincers* — an instrument with grasping jaws used to grip things

* *highwayman* — a person who robs travelers on a road

* *despoiled* — stripped of belongings or possessions

* *retinue* — attendants

* *blunderbusses* — a muzzle loading firearm

* *myriads* — great numbers

7 In paragraph 5, the author uses multiple semicolons in order to

A. contrast opposing ideas.

B. separate independent clauses.

C. show the chronological order of events.

D. signal for the reader to pay attention.

Ⓐ Ⓑ Ⓒ Ⓓ

Read the sentence from *A Tale of Two Cities* in the box below.

> It was the best of times, it was the worst of times, it was the age of wisdom, it was the age of foolishness, it was the epoch of belief, it was the epoch of incredulity, it was the season of Light, it was the season of Darkness. . . .

8 What is the purpose of the set of ellipses at the end of this excerpt?

A. to state the omission of more from the quoted passage

B. to intensify the speaker's thoughts about seasons

C. to prepare the reader for a new idea

D. to imply that the speaker is contradicting himself

Ⓐ Ⓑ Ⓒ Ⓓ

Read the sentence from *A Tale of Two Cities* in the box below.

> France, less favoured on the whole as to matters spiritual than her sister of the shield and trident, rolled with exceeding smoothness down the hill, making paper money and spending it.

9 Which of the following writing techniques does the sentence illustrate?

A. subordination

B. parallelism

C. metaphor

D. simile

Ⓐ Ⓑ Ⓒ Ⓓ

10 What does the dash in paragraph 1 indicate?

A. a change in thought

B. a summary

C. a shift in tone

D. a new idea

Ⓐ Ⓑ Ⓒ Ⓓ

11 In paragraph 3, the word *sublime* most likely comes from which of these origins?

A. Latin *sublimis*, uplifted

B. Latin *sibilare*, hissing

C. English *sublet*, to rent to another

D. Old French *subtil*, fine or delicate

Ⓐ Ⓑ Ⓒ Ⓓ

Read these lines from *A Tale of Two Cities* in the box below.

> There were a king with a large jaw and a queen with a plain face, on the throne of England; there were a king with a large jaw and a queen with a fair face, on the throne of France.

12 The author uses repetition here to show that

A. the countries were alike.

B. the countries were at war.

C. the two kings were related.

D. the situation was about to change.

Ⓐ Ⓑ Ⓒ Ⓓ

13 Who are the six characters mentioned and what is their relevance to one another in the following passage?

> Environed by them, while the Woodman and the Farmer worked unheeded, those of the large jaws, and those two of the plain and fair faces, trod with stir enough, and carried their divine rights with a high hand.

_____

_____

_____

_____

LESSON 3

Students will decode accurately and understand new words encountered in their reading materials, drawing on a variety of strategies as needed, and then use these words accurately in writing.

WHAT THIS STANDARD MEANS

For this standard, you have to understand words in the text to determine the meaning of these words or the text itself. You might be asked questions about details in the passage. You must be able to interpret the text to answer these questions correctly. Some questions may ask you to interpret words and phrases in the text that will be new to you or used in a way that you haven't seen before. For these questions, look at how the word or phrase is used in the sentence and try to figure out its meaning. Also read nearby sentences. You can often figure out the meaning of a new word by understanding how it is used in context.

STEP ONE | TEN-MINUTE LESSON

Sample Passage

OLD AS THE TREES IN NIAGARA

1 Despite the presence of hundreds of millions of curious tourists and photographers in the Niagara Falls area, botanists have only recently discovered what may be the oldest living trees in the northeastern United States. About 1,200 white cedar trees—believed to be at least 500 to 800 years old—were found clinging to the cliff walls of the U.S. and Canadian sides of the Niagara Gorge. (For comparison, the California redwoods average 800 to 1,500 years old.) Botanists believe they discovered the last of the cedars a few months ago after finding the first one in 1999. The trees measure as tall as 30 feet, and the trunks are 1 to 3 feet in diameter. Describing the tangled maze of branches, trunks, and surface roots, Bruce Kershner, a scientist and chairman of the Western New York Old Growth Forest Survey, says, "We realized the entire grove was a single clone, and what looked like multiple trees [was] really one tangled, interconnected organism. The scene actually felt and appeared alien, something you would expect to find on another planet." Douglas Larson, a botany professor at the University of Guelph in Ontario, says that the only way to accurately measure a tree's age is by increment coring—cutting samples from the trunk with a hollow drill bit. The Niagara Frontier Botanical Society plans to hire climbers to rappel down the cliff to measure the trees. Kershner says botanists were surprised to find these ancient virgin trees because, in addition to heavy tourism, cliff blasting and the building of a scenic railroad along the U.S. side have destroyed much of the area. Larson notes that European colonists even blew up forests in eastern North America, removing all forest cover, because the forests were seen as hazards to the settlers' survival.

Sample Questions

1 According to the article, how will botanists take samples of tree trunks to determine their age?

A. They will hire climbers to remove all forest cover.

B. They will hire climbers to measure the sizes of the trees.

C. They will hire climbers to measure the trees in the gorge.

D. They will hire climbers to untangle the maze of tree branches and roots.

Ⓐ Ⓑ Ⓒ Ⓓ

To answer this question, you need to go back to the article and reread the section that discusses how botanists measure the ages of trees. Then you need to read the sentences after that. What does it mean when the author says that climbers will measure the trees? The preceding sentences offer a clue.

Answer choice A: The article does say that the botanists will hire climbers, but not to remove forest cover. This is not the correct answer choice.

Answer choice B: The article says that the botanists will hire climbers to measure the trees, but not to measure their size. This is not the correct answer choice.

Answer choice C: The article says that the only way to measure a tree's age is by "cutting samples from the trunk with a hollow drill bit." These trees are growing in the sides of the Niagara Gorge. The climbers will climb into the gorge to take these samples. This seems to be the correct answer choice, but be sure to read all answer choices first.

Answer choice D: The article says that the trees are a tangled maze of roots and branches, but it does not say the climbers plan to untangle this maze. Therefore, this is not the correct answer choice. The best answer choice is C.

2 What did Bruce Kershner mean when he said that the "entire grove was one single clone"?

A. The trees in the grove looked the same.

B. They were able to clone the trees in the grove.

C. They entire grove was one type of tree.

D. The trees in the grove were really one tree.

Answer choice A: The trees in the grove looked the same, but if you read the rest of Bruce Kershner's quote, the trees were even more closely related. This is not the correct answer choice.

Answer choice B: The trees were clones, but the botanists were not cloning them. This is not the correct answer choice.

Answer choice C: The trees were one type of tree, but they were even more closely related. This is not the correct answer choice.

Answer choice D: If you read the entire quote, it tells you that what looked like multiple trees was really one tangled, interconnected organism. This means one tree. This is the correct answer choice.

3 In the passage, the word *rappel* means

A. move.

B. study.

C. slide down.

D. offer instruction.

Ⓐ Ⓑ Ⓒ Ⓓ

Answer choice A: The article says that the climbers will rappel down the cliff to measure the trees. This certainly means that they will move, but there might be a better answer choice.

Answer choice B: This is not the best answer choice since the article says that they will measure the trees. It doesn't say that they will study them.

Answer choice C: This answer choice seems correct, but read all answer choices first. The climbers will certainly have to slide down the cliff in order to measure the trees.

Answer choice D: Offering instruction is not mentioned in the article. Therefore, this is not the correct answer choice. Answer choice C is the correct choice.

Read the following passage. Then answer the questions. Use the Sidebar Instruction to help you choose the best answer.

from Kingdom of Coral

by Douglas H. Chadwick

1   AUSTRALIA'S GREAT BARRIER REEF—Sometimes at its outer edge and sometimes closer, the beam from the flashlight kept reflecting off big cat eyes. They glimmered pale silver, with pupils darker than the darkness through which they glided. But cats don't patrol 40 feet deep in the Coral Sea. These were sharks. It was hard to tell what kind they were, but some of the shadowy bodies looked a lot longer than mine.

2   I breathed up my scuba tank's air sooner than planned and had to surface far from the boat. Then I was swimming through black swells toward the ship's distant light as though mired in one of those dreams where you need to move faster but can't. I promised myself that it would be a while before my next night dive on Australia's Great Barrier Reef. Yet within days I was beneath a full moon and 50 feet of water looking at more cat eyes.

3   These belonged to an epaulette shark, small and lovely and speckled, lithe as an eel as it curled round a coral pillar. Two lionfish with fins like flared wing feathers cruised upside down beneath a coral table as though that were the seafloor. Above them a pinnacle of coral twisted nearly to the surface, lit from behind by the ship's lamps and the moon.

4   Silhouetted, each shelf, frond, curlicue, and fan emphasized the eerie configurations that develop in the near absence of gravity. Drifting weightless beside them seemed like sight-seeing on another planet. But the

moment I thought that, I realized that I had it wrong. This scene was the very essence of our home planet, which is, after all, ocean blue. A single coral wall holds a broader representation of earthly life—species from more phyla, or major groups—than an entire continent does. It seems otherworldly only to those of us born above tide line.

5 Coral reefs form when colonies of tropical marine plants and animals with limestone skeletons rise atop earlier generations. They fashion the most visually diverse natural environments a human can experience, and the Great Barrier Reef is the world's single largest coral domain. With the broad, shallow continental shelf of tropical northeastern Australia providing an ideal pedestal for growth, this coral complex reaches as far as 160 miles offshore and more than 1,250 miles from north to south. The Great Barrier Reef covers 135,000 square miles, an expanse greater than Poland.

6 To explore what amounts to an offshore nation, photographer David Doubilet and I roamed 4,000 miles on dive boats. We spent so many hours submerged that I began to think land looked weird. The day I found the same sort of remora fish that clings to sharks and manta rays hitching a ride on my leg, I wondered if it might not be time to dry out.

7 Although the name suggests a continuous strip, the Great Barrier Reef is actually a commonwealth of at least 2,800 reefs. Only some are true barrier reefs— breakwaters rising near the edge of the continental shelf. In the calmer seas behind that cordon, more reefs appear as irregular circles and crescents known as platform reefs. Smaller formations, called patch reefs, are scattered throughout shallow areas.

8 Fringing reefs grow outward from the mainland's shores, but more often they are found surrounding the region's 618 continental, or high, islands, which were mountains and hills along Australia's Ice Age coast before the glaciers melted and raised sea levels; the Aborigines' legends of ancient generations walking out to those islands are true. In addition there are about 300 low islands, or cays, formed atop coral shoals from reef sediments. As seabird droppings glue the grains together and colonizing plants build soil, some of those desert isles transform into shadowy woodlands, while storms pound others back into shifting piles of sand.

9 By acting as a buffer against heavy seas, the reef-and-island complex makes possible neighboring sea grass beds and coastal mangrove forests. Those in turn trap sediments, store nutrients, and serve as nurseries for a number of reef residents. Now add the soft sea bottoms between reefs plus submarine hillocks made entirely of Halimeda, a calcium-hardened green algae.

10 Put all these habitats together with clear azure waters flowing from the Coral Sea and brown, soil-laden waters washing off the continent. Mix with currents, daily tides, and seasonal weather patterns. What you have is the formula for the Great Barrier Reef ecosystem and lifetimes of discovery.

1 What are the "big cat eyes" the author refers to in the first paragraph?

A. lion's eyes

B. brightly colored coral

C. the Great Barrier Reef

D. shark's eyes

Ⓐ   Ⓑ   Ⓒ   Ⓓ

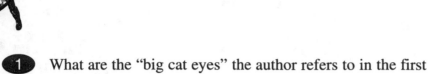

SIDEBAR INSTRUCTION
Reread the first paragraph. The author describes the eyes as "big cat eyes," but what are they really?

2 According to the article, how many reefs in the Great Barrier Reef are true barrier reefs?

A. only some of the reefs

B. all of the reefs

C. only one reef

D. those in irregular circles

Ⓐ   Ⓑ   Ⓒ   Ⓓ

SIDEBAR INSTRUCTION
Reread paragraph 7. What does it say about barrier reefs?

3 In paragraph 7, the term *commonwealth* refers to

A. a nation.

B. a union.

C. a merger.

V. a republic.

Ⓐ   Ⓑ   Ⓒ   Ⓓ

SIDEBAR INSTRUCTION
Find the word *commonwealth* in the paragraph. Then read the entire sentence. Which answer helps you understand the meaning of the word *commonwealth* as used in the sentence?

4 Which of the following lines from the article illustrates why the author enjoys spending time by the reef?

A. "Yet within days I was beneath a full moon and 50 feet of water looking at more cat eyes."

B. "A single coral wall holds a broader representation of earthly life—species from more phyla, or major groups— than an entire continent does."

C. "To explore what amounts to an offshore nation, photographer David Doubilet and I roamed 4,000 miles on dive boats."

D. "Then I was swimming through black swells toward the ship's distant light as though mired in one of those dreams where you need to move faster but can't."

Ⓐ Ⓑ Ⓒ Ⓓ

SIDEBAR INSTRUCTION
Read the answer choices carefully. Choose the one that best shows that the author enjoys diving by the Great Barrier Reef.

5 According to the article, when did the author think it was time to get out of the water?

A. when a remora fish was clinging to his leg

B. when a shark was close by him

C. when a manta ray was clinging to his leg

D. when he thought land looked weird

Ⓐ Ⓑ Ⓒ Ⓓ

SIDEBAR INSTRUCTION
Reread the part of the article when the author wonders if it is time to dry out. What makes him think this?

6 What does the last line of the article suggest to the reader?

A. Many other coral reefs will be discovered in the future.

B. There is still more to learn about coral reefs.

C. In the future, people will discover how to grow coral reefs.

D. We need to encourage more people to explore coral reefs.

Ⓐ   Ⓑ   Ⓒ   Ⓓ

SIDEBAR INSTRUCTION
Reread the last line and think about its meaning.

7 What does the author learn about the eerie configurations of the Great Barrier Reef? Use relevant and specific information from the essay to support your answer.

_____

_____

_____

_____

_____

_____

_____

_____

STEP THREE ON YOUR OWN

Read the following passage. Then answer the questions.

Forget crackers—
what Polly
wants is
a vacation

by Daniel Pinkwater

1   To this day, I have a way with parrots, and sometimes will take a friend into a pet shop where I can show off by relating to the birds, calming the frantic ones, getting others to talk and coo suggestively, and offer their heads to be scratched. I have even picked up my father's trick—for which my hands were too small in the old days—of taking a punishing beak between my knuckles and engaging in a kind of tug-of-war that parrots seem to appreciate.

2   None of this should be taken to suggest that I like parrots, macaws, cockatoos, cockatiels, parakeets, lorikeets, African love-birds or any of that disagreeable bunch. My idea of cruel and unusual punishment would be to be confined in a small space with a parrot—hell would be confinement with a whole lot of them. All my life, I've avoided every place on Earth where hook-billed seed-eaters fly wild.

3   As a child, I did not know I hated parrots, just that my father loved them. In Chicago, right after World War II, few people had parrots, but my father managed to find a redheaded Panama that he named Pedro.

4   Each day, a half-hour before my father was due to return from work, Pedro would begin shrieking, flapping and hyperventilating. By the time my father came through the door, Pedro would have worked himself into a fit. His feathers awry, his pupils dilating and contracting, he'd be hanging upside down, making little psychotic cooing noises.

5   My father would cradle Pedro in his arms, arranging his feathers and comforting him. "Dot's a good boid," he would say, "a good boid."

6   Pedro fell ill. And the boiler gave out during Pedro's crisis. Keep him warm and give him stimulants, the vet said. I remember this scene: Pedro wrapped in a dish towel, tucked up, immobilized, in a black enamel roasting pan. My father had Pedro resting on the open oven

door and was in the act of pouring Scotch down Pedro's beak out of a shot glass. The stricken Pedro was looking around wildly.

7 I figure the bird died of fear as much as anything else. Somewhat to my surprise, I took it hard when Pedro pegged out. My father did too. We spent a long time sitting in the darkened living room, being miserable and weeping. "Sonnyeh," my father sniffed, "don't you vorry, boy. We'll hev more parrots—lots of parrots."

8 "Or maybe we'll just get a dog?" I whimpered, snuggling up to my father.

9 "Naw, Sonnyeh, you don't hev to settle for a dog. I'll get you planty parrots, vait and see."

10 And so he did. I became fairly proficient in dealing with scaly leg mites, wing clipping, creating nutritious mixtures of seeds and grain, and the many psychological disorders peculiar to parrots, including the common one of idly plucking out their own feathers until they look like dressed chickens on the hoof.

11 About this time, my parents discovered a new form of diversion. At the onset of winter, we would entrain for California.

12 The family must have made an unforgettable picture as we made ready to board the Super Chief in Chicago. A single-file procession: first, my father, wearing his powder-blue suit, Stetson and topcoat, carrying over his shoulder the brown leather case containing his Cine-Kodak, and in hand, a huge Zenith portable radio in the shape of a suitcase and featuring the patented Wave Magnet antenna. My mother would follow, in her furpiece, clutching a few magazines. Next in line, myself, bearing two wooden traveling cases chock-full of parakeets, and bringing up the rear, looking as though she wanted to die, my sister Isabel, bearing still another box containing a parrot or two.

13 My father would have booked a double drawing room, and once we were rolling, we would spread out and get comfortable. The powerful Zenith would be fired up, the Wave Magnet stuck to the window with suction cups, so we could listen to H. V. Kaltenborn, "It Pays To Be Ignorant" and other favorites. My father would relax behind a newspaper. The traveling boxes would be opened, and the birds would flutter and perch here and there about the compartment. I would sprawl on the floor, absorbed in a comic book. My mother might knit, and Isabel would fixate on the pages of Gardner's *Art Through the Ages*, probably fantasizing that she was traveling in another country, and alone.

14 Pullman porters would bring ice-cold 7-Up, the family's favorite traveling beverage. And so we would rattle through the night, oblivious (except for Isabel) of our profound abnormality, heading for a winter beneath the palms.

15 In time, the parrot craze diminished. The parakeets and lesser Psittaciformes went, I know not where. They may have died off or been given away—I don't recall. We wound up with one parrot, Lucky—a fairly mellow Panama, by far the least obnoxious of all the birds we'd owned. My father left Lucky in the care of my sister Helen, who lived in California, when we left for home at the end of one winter. Helen hung Lucky's cage on her patio. He picked the lock one day and headed for Mexico. "God bless him," Isabel said, when we got the news. "I hope he makes it."

7 What does the author mean when he says that Pedro "pegged out"?

A. Pedro became sick.

B. Pedro fell asleep.

C. Pedro died.

D. Pedro froze.

Ⓐ Ⓑ Ⓒ Ⓓ

8 According to the article, how were the author and his family different from other travelers?

A. They drank 7-Up on the trip.

B. They carried birds.

C. They had a double drawing room.

D. They read magazines.

Ⓐ Ⓑ Ⓒ Ⓓ

9 Which of the following lines from the article shows that Lucky escaped from his cage?

A. "My father left Lucky in the care of my sister Helen, who lived in California, when we left for home at the end of one winter."

B. "He picked the lock one day and headed for Mexico."

C. "They may have died off or been given away—I don't recall."

D. "In time, the parrot craze diminished."

Ⓐ Ⓑ Ⓒ Ⓓ

10 When the author says in paragraph 15 that the "parrot craze diminished," he means that

A. parrots became difficult to find.

B. the parrots were stolen.

C. his father stopped keeping parrots.

D. his father no longer liked parrots.

Ⓐ Ⓑ Ⓒ Ⓓ

11 Paragraph 9 shows that

A. the author's father was not educated.

B. the author's father spoke broken English.

C. the author had trouble remembering what his father said.

D. the author enjoyed imitating his father's speech.

Ⓐ Ⓑ Ⓒ Ⓓ

12 What does the author say probably contributed to Pedro's illness?

A. His father wrapped him in a dish towel.

B. The boiler broke while he was sick.

C. His father put him in a roasting pan.

D. The vet gave him stimulants.

Ⓐ Ⓑ Ⓒ Ⓓ

13 How is the essay's title "Forget crackers—what Polly wants is a vacation" related to the theme? Support your answer with details and information from the essay.

_____

_____

_____

_____

_____

_____

_____

This section reviews the standards you have just learned. The questions in this review are for Standards 4, 5, and 8.

Founding Father's Right Touch

Word Whiz: Thomas Jefferson topped his works with Declaration of Independence

by Michael Mink

1   Thomas Jefferson wanted answers. Oncc hc had onc, he made sure he knew where to find it again.

2   A voracious reader, Jefferson kept a library of more than 9,000 books. He took copious notes on what he studied, including science, horticulture, farming, architecture and astronomy, and kept copies of his voluminous correspondence. All was organized so he could find it at a moment's notice.

3   Why? Because Jefferson (1743–1826) cherished learning and discovery.

4   "One of Jefferson's eulogists said after he died, 'Anything he didn't know the answer to, he knew where to find the answer,'" said Lucia Stanton, a senior research historian at Monticello, Jefferson's home in Virginia.

5   Jefferson, the nation's third president and author of the Declaration of Independence, admired the writings and ideals of such Enlightenment thinkers as Francis Bacon, Isaac Newton, John Locke and Thomas Paine. What he learned and retained from them greatly influenced his own work.

6   "I did not consider it as any part of my charge to invent new ideas altogether, and to offer no sentiment which had ever been expressed before," Jefferson said about his work on the Declaration of Independence.

Everything In Its Place

7   In his great library at Monticello, ("I cannot live without books," he said,) Jefferson carefully arranged his manuscripts in categories and subcategories, said Jack Robertson, the Jefferson Foundation librarian at Monticello.

8   Doing this let Jefferson "always remember a thought or a quote in terms of the specific author, the specific book, and where that book fit in the large intellectual landscape that was the Enlightenment, the 18th century," Robertson said.

9   To jog his memory later, Jefferson wrote down much of what he learned in his farm and memorandum books. "Nothing was so ordinary or taken for granted that it could escape his scrutiny or his questioning," wrote Johanna Johnston in "Thomas Jefferson: His Many Talents."

10   His notes were more than lists. He also analyzed everything he saw.

11   "He kept minute written detail of seeds and plants and how they performed," Robertson said. "He kept track of performance so he could revise what he planted and where he planted. Jefferson was forever experimenting. . . . He was forever trying to push the boundaries (of discovery). That's part of what he did with the Lewis and Clark expedition."

12   Jefferson had a daily routine to keep him on track. He began his days early to get a jump-start on his many activities. "I rise with the sun," he said.

13   In a letter, he advised his grandson: "Rise at a fixed and an early hour, and go to bed at a fixed and early hour also. Sitting up late at night is injurious to the health, and not useful to the mind."

14   "Jefferson was a fervent believer in making a daily habit of actions that reward us with wisdom, health and happiness," wrote Coy Barefoot in "Thomas Jefferson on Leadership."

15   Staying busy helps one manage time and accomplish more, Jefferson believed. So he kept his days heavily scheduled, and urged others to do the same. "Determine never to be idle. No person will have occasion to complain of the want of time, who never loses any. It is wonderful how much may be done, if we are always doing," Jefferson wrote in a letter to his daughter.

Time Alone

16   A prolific writer (he wrote some 20,000 letters in his lifetime), Jefferson realized that he worked better when he could focus on a task for a longer period. So he set aside each morning as his "alone time."

17   "He would be uninterrupted basically from breakfast until the middle of the afternoon," Stanton said. "I think most of us allow our days to get chopped up into little pieces, but he kept this long stretch of time when he was in his study doing his writing or architectural drawing or his other mind work. Mornings were his mental time."

18   Jefferson devoted the middle of each day to physical activity. Walking, he said, was "the best possible exercise." He believed exercise was essential to keeping the mind alert and active. "Exercise and recreation are as necessary as reading; I will say rather more necessary . . . a strong body makes the mind strong," Jefferson said.

19   The rest of Jefferson's day was spent with family and social activities. Realizing that "one of the first tasks of responsible leaders is to focus their efforts on self-improvement," he would spend time reading every evening, Barefoot said.

20   "I never go to bed without an hour, or half hour's previous reading of something moral, whereon to ruminate in the intervals of sleep," Jefferson wrote in a letter.

21   Jefferson wasn't after only self-improvement. Every step he took to better himself, he believed, added "to the stock of human knowledge," Stanton wrote. "In the Enlightenment, there was such faith in human reason and knowledge and belief that it would improve the whole human condition. That was Jefferson's driving force throughout his life. Every little detail he wrote down, I think he felt on some level 'I'm making the world a better place by doing this.' "

22   Not everyone had the money to travel the way Jefferson did, and he knew it. So when he traveled, he wrote down everything he saw and experienced with an eye toward sharing it with others. After returning from trips through France and Italy, "he used to read aloud from that journal to his friends in Philadelphia, for their edification," Stanton said. "So a lot of what he was doing in terms of record keeping over there was to help the United States at whatever it was, whether it was to make better canals or learning to make Parmesan cheese."

An Educated Populace

23   People need as much information as possible to make good decisions, Jefferson knew, especially when it came to government. "Every government degenerates when trusted to the rulers of the people alone. The people themselves, therefore, are its only safe depositors," he wrote. "And to render even them safe, their minds must be improved to a certain degree."

24   Jefferson understood that firsthand knowledge is the most accurate, and he strove to gather his own information. He also knew he couldn't be everywhere at once.

25   When he was president, for example, he asked his Cabinet officers to send him a daily packet consisting of the letters they received that day, and their responses, wrote Noble Cunningham in "In Pursuit of Reason: The Life of Thomas Jefferson." That way he got the story upfront and didn't have to depend on others to interpret events.

26   As usual, "(Jefferson) said he expected to be 'always in accurate possession of all facts and proceedings,' " Cunningham wrote.

1 What does the word *copius* mean in paragraph 2?

A. abstract

B. secretive

C. numerous

D. approximate

Ⓐ Ⓑ Ⓒ Ⓓ

2 In paragraph 2, the word *voracious* means

A. brilliant.

B. avid.

C. notorious.

D. exceptional.

Ⓐ Ⓑ Ⓒ Ⓓ

3 In paragraph 9, the word *scrutiny* means

A. confusion

B. examination

C. determination

D. objection

Ⓐ Ⓑ Ⓒ Ⓓ

4 In paragraph 21 of the article, what does the phrase "driving force" mean?

A. favorite activity

B. most serious problem

C. biggest supporter

D. primary motivation

Ⓐ Ⓑ Ⓒ Ⓓ

5 Why does the author include only two sentences in paragraph 10?

A. to serve as an introduction to a new idea

B. to emphasize the importance of these ideas

C. to compare and contrast Jefferson's habits

D. to identify Jefferson's own ideas

Ⓐ Ⓑ Ⓒ Ⓓ

6 What does the word *fervent* mean in paragraph 14?

A. indifferent

B. particular

C. encouraging

D. strong

Ⓐ Ⓑ Ⓒ Ⓓ

7 What does the word *prolific* mean in paragraph 16?

A. productive

B. exceptional

C. underestimated

D. renown

Ⓐ Ⓑ Ⓒ Ⓓ

8 What does the word *edification* mean in paragraph 22?

A. approval

B. displeasure

C. justification

D. enlightenment

Ⓐ Ⓑ Ⓒ Ⓓ

9 Jefferson wrote the following in a letter to his daughter. Using relevant and specific information from the essay, how does Jefferson practice what he preaches?

> Determine never to be idle. No person will have occasion to complain of the want of time who never loses any. It is wonderful how much may be done if we are always doing.

_____

_____

_____

_____

_____

_____

_____

_____

10 Use information from the selection to support this line from one of Jefferson's eulogists.

> Anything he didn't know the answer to, he knew where to find the answer.

_____

_____

_____

_____

_____

_____

_____

_____

_____

_____

LESSON 4

Students will identify the basic facts and essential ideas in what they have read, heard, or viewed.

WHAT THIS STANDARD MEANS

Questions assessing this benchmark will ask you to remember important details in a passage. You might have to go back and reread the passage or parts of the passage to answer these questions.

STEP ONE **TEN-MINUTE LESSON**

Sample Passage

Golden Girl: Olympic Swimmer Megan Quann

National Geographic World

1   Stroke, stroke, breathe, stroke. Megan Quann moved through the water as fast as a seal, but she was still behind in the most important race of her life. She'd have to swim harder. Stroke, pull, faster. Now the finish! But who won? Her eyes flashed to the scoreboard to read: "1. Megan Quann, U.S.A." Yes? Megan, 16, had just won—by a split second—the gold medal in the 100-meter breaststroke at last summer's 2000 Olympic Games in Sydney, Australia. "I don't worry about anyone else," she said afterward. "I focus on me and the water." Days later Megan won another gold medal swimming on the women's 400-meter medley relay team, which took first place and also set a world record.

2   Back to school. Megan is a winner at high school, too, where she earns a 3.8 grade point average. "I don't take physical education class, but I get credit for going to the Olympics. My principal joked that he'd give me an A in P. E. if I medaled."

3   Goals. Training still fills 35 hours a week, which is fine with this super-achiever. "I'm never satisfied," says Megan, who wants to go to college, break the world record in the breaststroke, and swim in two more Olympics. She loves the thrill of winning for her country: "It's the biggest honor ever."

Sample Questions

1 In this selection, what does Megan say about her principal?

A. He was her most dedicated supporter.

B. He made a joke about her physical education grade.

C. He advised her to focus on the water.

D. He told her to train thirty-five hours a week.

Ⓐ Ⓑ Ⓒ Ⓓ

This question asks you to recall a detail from the selection you've just read. Remember, you can refer back to the passage. If you don't know the answer to the question, look back and try to find the answer in the passage. Also, be sure to read all your choices before deciding.

Answer choice A: Was Megan's principal also her most dedicated supporter? Think about what Megan said in the selection. She did not mention any particular supporters. The principal may have been her most dedicated supporter, but this information was not included in the selection. This is not the correct answer choice.

Answer choice B: Think about what you read in the passage. Megan told about how her principal joked that he'd give her an A in physical education if she won a medal. This appears to be the correct choice, but be sure to read the next choices just to make sure.

Answer choice C: Did Megan's principal advise her to focus on the water? Think about what the swimmer said in the passage. She said that her strategy was to focus on herself and the water. She did not say the principal gave her that advice. Answer choice B is a better answer.

Answer choice D: The passage says that Megan trained thirty-five hours a week, but it doesn't say her principal told her to do this. Answer choice B is the correct answer.

2 How did Megan learn she had won her first gold medal?

A. She watched her team win first place.

B. She received an A in physical education.

C. She saw the other swimmers behind her.

D. She saw her name on the scoreboard.

Ⓐ   Ⓑ   Ⓒ   Ⓓ

Answer choice A: Read the question carefully. The selection explains that Megan did win a gold medal when her women's 400-meter medley relay team took first place. However, that was her second gold medal. The question asks about her first gold medal, so there is probably a better answer choice.

Answer choice B: The selection said that the principal joked that he would give her an A in physical education. Even if he did this, it was not how Megan first learned about her win. You can eliminate this choice.

Answer choice C: Did Megan look back during the race and see her competitors behind her? She may have done this, but the selection does not mention it. There is a better answer choice.

Answer choice D: Look back to the selection. The first paragraph explains that Megan was uncertain about whether she had won until she saw her name in the number one spot on the scoreboard. So, answer choice D is the correct answer.

STEP TWO SIDEBAR INSTRUCTION

**Read the passage and answer the questions that follow. Use the Sidebar Instruction
to help you choose the best answer.**

from
THE NO-GUITAR
BLUES

by Gary Soto

1   The moment Fausto saw the group Los Lobos on "American Bandstand," he knew exactly what he wanted to do with his life—play guitar. His eyes grew large with excitement as Los Lobos ground out a song while teenagers bounced off each other on the crowded dance floor.

2   He had watched "American Bandstand" for years and had heard Ray Carmacho and the Teardrops at Romain Playground, but it had never occurred to him that he too might become a musician. That afternoon Fausto knew his mission in life: to play guitar in his own band; to sweat out his songs and prance around the stage; to make money and dress weird.

3   Fausto turned off the television set and walked outside, wondering how he could get enough money to buy a guitar. He couldn't ask his parents because they would just say, "Money doesn't grow on trees" or "What do you think we are, bankers?"

And besides, they hated rock music. They were into *conjunto** music of Ludia Mendoza, Flaco Jimenez, and Little Joe and La Familia. And, as Fausto recalled, the last album they bought was *The Chipmunks Sing Christmas Favorites*.

4   But what the heck, he'd give it a try. He returned inside and watched his mother make tortillas. He leaned against the kitchen counter, trying to work up the nerve to ask her for a guitar. Finally, he couldn't hold back any longer.

5   "Mom," he said, "I want a guitar for Christmas."

6   She looked up from rolling tortillas. "Honey, a guitar costs a lot of money."

7   "How 'bout for my birthday next year," he tried again.

8   "I can't promise," she said, turning back to her tortillas, "but we'll see."

9   Fausto walked back outside with a buttered tortilla. He knew his mother was

85

right. His father was a warehouseman at Berven Rugs, where he made good money but not enough to buy everything his children wanted. Fausto decided to mow lawns to earn money, and was pushing the mower down the street before he realized it was winter and no one would hire him. He returned the mower and picked up a rake. He hopped onto his sister's bike (his had two flat tires) and rode north to the nicer section of Fresno in search of work. He went door-to-door, but after three hours he managed to get only one job, and not to rake leaves. He was asked to hurry down to the store to buy a loaf of bread, for which he received a grimy, dirt-caked quarter.

10   He also got an orange, which he ate sitting at the curb. While he was eating, a dog walked up and sniffed his leg. Fausto pushed him away and threw an orange peel skyward. The dog caught it and ate it in one gulp. The dog looked at Fausto and wagged his tail for more. Fausto tossed him a slice of orange, and the dog snapped it up and licked his lips.

11   "How come you like oranges, dog?"

12   The dog blinked a pair of sad eyes and whined.

13   "What's the matter? Cat got your tongue?" Fausto laughed at his joke and offered the dog another slice.

14   At that moment a dim light came on inside Fausto's head. He saw that it was a sort of fancy dog, a terrier or something, with dog tags and a shiny collar. And it looked well fed and healthy. In his neighborhood, the dogs were never licensed, and if they got sick they were placed near the water heater until they got well.

15   This dog looked like he belonged to rich people. Fausto cleaned his juice-sticky hands on his pants and got to his feet. The light in his head grew brighter. It just might work. He called the dog, patted its muscular back, and bent down to check the license.

16   "Great," he said. "There's an address."

17   The dog's name was Roger, which struck Fausto as weird because he'd never heard of a dog with a human name. Dogs should have names like Bomber, Freckles, Queenie, Killer, and Zero.

18   Fausto planned to take the dog home and collect a reward. He would say he had found Roger near the freeway. That would scare the daylights out of the owners, who would be so happy that they would probably give him a reward. He felt bad about lying, but the dog *was* loose. And it might even really be lost, because the address was six blocks away.

---

* conjunto – a type of Latin American dance band

1 What was Fausto's first plan to earn money?

A. to return a lost dog

B. to mow lawns

C. to rake leaves

D. to deliver groceries

Ⓐ Ⓑ Ⓒ Ⓓ

SIDEBAR INSTRUCTION
This story tells several of Fausto's moneymaking plans. Read the question carefully. Which of these plans came first?

2 Why did Fausto decide to become a musician?

A. He wanted to rebel against his parents.

B. He loved listening to *conjunto* music.

C. His parents were also musicians.

D. He saw a musical group on television.

Ⓐ Ⓑ Ⓒ Ⓓ

SIDEBAR INSTRUCTION
The beginning of this selection explains the reason Fausto wanted to be a musician. If you don't remember the reason, refer back to the selection.

3 According to the selection, why did Fausto go to the north side of Fresno in search of work?

A. He wanted to travel to a new place.

B. He didn't want his sister to see him on her bike.

C. The people on the north side of Fresno had more money.

D. The people on the north side of Fresno were very friendly.

Ⓐ Ⓑ Ⓒ Ⓓ

SIDEBAR INSTRUCTION
The story tells why Fausto thought working on the north side of Fresno would be ideal. Reread the story if you can't remember.

4 What did Fausto feed the dog?

A. buttered tortillas

B. his dinner

C. an orange

D. bread

Ⓐ Ⓑ Ⓒ Ⓓ

SIDEBAR INSTRUCTION
This story mentions several types of food. When Fausto finds the dog, what food does he share with it?

5 Why can't Fausto have a guitar?

    A. His parents don't like rock music.

    B. His parents don't have enough money.

    C. His mother wants him to get a job.

    D. His father has lost his job.

    Ⓐ Ⓑ Ⓒ Ⓓ

SIDEBAR INSTRUCTION
Reread the part of the story where Fausto asks his mother if he can have a guitar. What is her response?

6 Why does Fausto decide to return the dog?

    A. The dog is near the freeway.

    B. The dog eats his food.

    C. Fausto is hoping for a reward.

    D. Fausto thinks the dog is lost.

    Ⓐ Ⓑ Ⓒ Ⓓ

SIDEBAR INSTRUCTION
Reread the end of the story. What plan does Fausto devise involving the return of the dog?

7 In your own words, trace the plot of "The No-Guitar Blues."

_____

_____

_____

_____

_____

_____

_____

_____

_____

STEP THREE ON YOUR OWN

Read the passage. Then answer the questions that follow.

The Mighty Conestoga

by Lisa Mullins Bishop

1   The Conestoga wagon was the eighteen-wheeler of its day, transporting freight overland. Drawn by four or six powerful draft horses, the boat-shaped, covered Conestoga could haul four to six tons of cargo—everything from cloth, tea and teapots, and spices to nails and gunpowder.

2   In the early eighteenth century, they carried produce from the farms around Lancaster, Pennsylvania, to the markets in Philadelphia and Baltimore. The sixty-three-mile journey from Lancaster to Philadelphia, a trip that took four days over rough roads, called for a strong wagon with a protective cover. Soon the useful vehicle was pressed into government service: it carried supplies to General Edward Braddock and his troops near Pittsburgh during the French and Indian War and to General George Washington at Valley Forge. After the Revolution, Conestogas became a common sight on the country's roads. In 1789, Benjamin Rush noted that "it is not uncommon to meet in one day from fifty to a hundred of these waggons* on their way to Philadelphia."

3   With the Treaty of Paris, England ceded the land beyond the Appalachian Mountains to the new nation, and settlers began entering the Ohio Valley in large numbers. The Conestoga wagon became their link with city markets, its distinctive shape and construction well suited to the rough, steep terrain they followed. There were three main routes: over the Appalachian Mountains to Pittsburgh, where the freight was then shipped downriver into the Ohio Valley; along the National Road connecting Baltimore and Frederick, Maryland, with Wheeling, West Virginia, the other gateway to the Ohio Valley; and down the Great Wagon Road through the Valley of Virginia into North Carolina. These wagon trails became our highways.

4   Pennsylvania Germans living in the Conestoga River Valley near Lancaster created the Conestoga wagon, basing it on

early English and German models. Like most things they made, it was beautiful as well as practical, with a graceful, boatlike shape that distinguished it from other wagons in appearance and usefulness. It consisted of two separate parts: the wagon and the undercarriage, or running gear. The wagon bed generally measured sixteen feet long, four feet wide, and three feet deep and sloped upward at both ends to prevent cargo from shifting on steep terrain; gates at either end secured the cargo inside. A white cover of canvas, sailcloth, or homespun hemp stretched over six to thirteen wooden hoops or bows to protect and conceal the cargo. Instead of being affixed to its undercarriage, the wagon bed touched the running gear at only three points, making it flexible for traversing rocky roads. Two large wheels in back and two smaller ones in front increased the wagon's stability, as did their four-inch iron rims. In keeping with the Pennsylvania Germans' penchant for vivid color, the wagon was painted bright blue; the undercarriage red.

5   Wagoners prided themselves on both their wagons and their teams. Two or three pairs of powerful yet docile horses, also known as Conestogas, were outfitted with expensive harnesses and bells of varied tones—five small bells on the lead team, four bells on the middle, and four large on the rear team. These bells became a symbol of status, and it was considered shameful for any driver to arrive at his destination without his bells. (This is probably the origin of the saying, "I'll be there with bells on.")

6   Hauling freight paid well. In 1786 the rate for hauling freight from Philadelphia to Pittsburgh was five pence per pound; most Conestogas could haul thousands of pounds. A driver loaded his wagon with as much cargo as it could hold, up to the bows in many cases. Instead of riding in the wagon, he walked alongside it. If he didn't want to walk, he could ride on the left rear horse or sit on the lazy-board, a wooden board that pulled out from the wagon, precariously located in front of the left rear wheel. The wagoner controlled the horses through a single rein that ran on the left side of the team, not the divided reins common on other wagons. They were the first to drive their teams from the left, just as Americans drive their cars today.

7   The Conestoga wagon held everything a wagoner needed. A toolbox with a slanted lid was built into the exterior on the left side; stored inside was equipment for shoeing the horses, trimming hooves, repairing harnesses and the wagon. A feedbox, measuring five to six feet long, twelve inches wide, and ten inches deep, was built into the rear. Because the wheels needed to be removed every hundred miles so the axles could be greased, a wagon jack, a tar pot, and an iron hook for hanging it were standard equipment. Each wagon also carried a water bucket for the horses and an ax.

8   The work of a wheelwright and a blacksmith, a wagon took two months to build and cost about two hundred dollars. James Sorber, an iron collector who has made Conestoga-related iron a specialty, says the wagoner spent more money on ironwork than anything else on the wagon. That each wagoner tried to outdo the other is evident from the ornately decorated toolboxes, whose wrought-iron hasps and hinges were in the form of decorative burning bushes, rams' heads, and tulips. The blacksmith's skill wasn't limited to these; the hounds that braced and connected parts of the wagon, hub caps, chains, ax holder, and wagon jack were as much works of art as they were necessities. Today they are eagerly sought and highly prized by iron collectors.

---

* waggon – early spelling of wagon

8 Approximately how long did it take to build a Conestoga wagon?

A. two days

B. two weeks

C. two months

D. two years

Ⓐ   Ⓑ   Ⓒ   Ⓓ

9 According to the article, the Conestoga wagon was used like what modern vehicle?

A. an eighteen-wheeler

B. a dump truck

C. a boat

D. a tank

Ⓐ   Ⓑ   Ⓒ   Ⓓ

10 What well-known saying likely originated among wagoners?

A. "You can count on me."

B. "That's the ticket!"

C. "I'll be there with bells on."

D "I'm so hungry I could eat a horse."

Ⓐ   Ⓑ   Ⓒ   Ⓓ

11 Who usually worked together to build Conestoga wagons?

A. Pennsylvania Germans and Britons

B. wheelwrights and blacksmiths

C. farmers and merchants

D soldiers and villagers

Ⓐ   Ⓑ   Ⓒ   Ⓓ

12 According to the article, what happened to the first wagon trails?

A. They were abandoned and forgotten.

B. People planted flowers and trees along them.

C. They were converted into highways.

D. They are now national parks.

Ⓐ   Ⓑ   Ⓒ   Ⓓ

13 What was the purpose of the white canvas cover on the wagon?

A. to block out rain

B. to keep the riders cool

C. to protect the cargo

D. to hold the bows together

Ⓐ   Ⓑ   Ⓒ   Ⓓ

14 According to the article, where was the wagoner of a Conestoga during travel?

A. walking alongside it

B. sitting on the right front horse

C. sitting on a bench in front

D. perched on top of the cargo

Ⓐ Ⓑ Ⓒ Ⓓ

15 What was the "Mighty Conestoga" and what purpose did it serve? Use relevant details and information from the passage.

_____

_____

_____

_____

_____

_____

_____

_____

_____

LESSON 5

Students will identify, analyze, and apply knowledge of the characteristics of different genres.

WHAT THIS STANDARD MEANS

Questions assessed by this benchmark will ask you to identify different types of literature. You may be asked to identify and analyze the characteristics of various genres. You may also be asked where a passage would most likely be found.

STEP ONE | TEN-MINUTE LESSON

Sample Passage

Sea otter plan praised after delay

by Don Thompson

1   A long-awaited sea otter recovery plan blames human activities for the decline in the California sea otter population. It raises the threshold for when the animal can be removed from federal protection.

2   The plan by the U.S. Fish and Wildlife Service comes after 16 years of delays and false starts. It's been 21 years since the previous plan was presented.

3   The new plan recommends reducing oil spills, ocean pollutants and entanglements with boat motors and fishing gear.

4   It also calls for more research to determine why otters haven't recovered after being named a threatened species in 1977. And it sets higher thresholds for when the population could be considered safe enough to be removed from federal Endangered Species Act protection.

5   Environmentalists praised the plan for including recommendations they'd been making for years.

6   "At long last, we have a blueprint for the recovery of otters," said Jim Curland, of Defenders of Wildlife.

7   The new plan says the otter population would have to reach 8,400 animals before the species would be no longer listed under the Marine Mammal Protection Act.

8   Otters were hunted nearly to extinction for their soft pelts by the early 20th century. They reached a population high of 2,377 in 1995. Since then, the population has dropped to about 2,150 animals.

9   The decline has been an unsolved mystery to scientists, who are struggling to save the species from extinction.

Sample Questions

 1 Where would you most likely find this selection?

A. a dictionary

B. a biography

C. a newspaper

D. an atlas

Ⓐ   Ⓑ   Ⓒ   Ⓓ

This question asks you to decide where this selection would best fit. Think about what this selection says and what kinds of information it has. This will help you decide what genre, or type of writing, it is. Now, where does it best belong?

Answer choice A: Does this selection belong in a dictionary? Dictionaries give facts and information, just like this selection does. Because this article contains quotes and dated information, it would not be in a dictionary.

Answer choice B: Is this selection an example of a biography? Think about what you know about biographies. This selection does include some information on people's lives and ideas, but it is mostly about the sea otter recovery plan. You can eliminate this answer choice.

Answer choice C: Would you likely find this selection in a newspaper? Newspapers contain facts, figures, quotes, and dated information. This article includes all of those items. It is written in newspaper style for quick reading and understanding. This is probably the best answer choice, but be sure to read all the choices before choosing.

Answer choice D: Is this selection an example of the writing in an atlas? Think about what writing you might find in an atlas. An atlas contains maps and geographical information. This selection doesn't include information on those topics. This is not the best answer. Answer choice C is the correct answer.

2 What is the intention of this article?

A. to inform readers of the sea otter recovery plan

B. to urge readers to assist in the sea otter recovery plan

C. to make readers angry about sea otter hunting

D. to give detailed information to other researchers to read

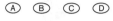
Ⓐ   Ⓑ   Ⓒ   Ⓓ

Now that you've thought about what genre, or category of writing this is and where it would best fit, this question asks you to go a step further. What is this selection meant to accomplish? Think about what you've already concluded about the selection. What is its primary purpose?

Answer choice A: Is the purpose of this selection to inform people about a new recovery plan? Think about what you've read in the selection. It talks about a problem and then a possible solution to the problem. It contains facts, figures, quotes, and timely information. It does inform the reader, so this is probably the best choice. However, you should check the other choices just to make sure.

Answer choice B: The author of this selection may want more people to assist in the sea otter recovery plan, but he does not mention it. This isn't the main purpose of the selection.

Answer choice C: The author might want people to be upset about the decline in the sea otter population. He or she does not mention this in the selection, though. The author is just reporting facts and quotes, so this is not the best answer choice.

Answer choice D: Is this selection meant to give detailed information to other researchers? Think about what you've read. It does give a lot of information, and it may seem like detailed information. However, a researcher would probably need more information than is provided in this selection to get a full understanding of sea otters. This is probably not the best answer choice. The best answer choice is A.

3 What is one device the author uses in this article?

A. autobiographical info

B. question and answer

C. statistical information

D. survey results

Answer choice A: If a passage contains autobiographical information, an author tells about his or her life. The author does not do this in this passage, so this is not the correct answer choice.

Answer choice B: This article does not contain questions and answers, so this is not the correct answer choice.

Answer choice C: Statistical information involves facts and numbers. This passage does give statistical information about the number of sea otters. This is probably the best answer choice, but you should read and consider answer choice D to be certain.

Answer choice D: The author does not discuss a survey in this passage, so this is not the best answer choice. Answer choice C is the correct answer.

STEP TWO SIDEBAR INSTRUCTION

Read the selection and answer the questions that follow. Use the Sidebar Instruction to help you choose the correct answer.

from Men at Work

by Anna Quindlen

1   Overheard in a Manhattan restaurant, one woman to another:

2   "He's a terrific father, but he's never home."

3   The five o'clock dads can be seen on cable television these days, just after that time in the evening the stay-at-home moms call the arsenic hours. They are sixties sitcom reruns, Ward and Steve and Alex, and fifties guys. They eat dinner with their television families and provide counsel afterward in the den. Someday soon, if things keep going the way they are, their likenesses will be enshrined in a diorama at the Museum of National History, frozen in their recliner chairs. The sign will say, "Here sit lifelike representations of family men who worked only eight hours a day."

4   The five o'clock dad has become an endangered species. A corporate culture that believes presence is productivity, in which people of ambition are afraid to be seen leaving the office, has lengthened his workday and shortened his homelife. So has an economy that makes it difficult for families to break even at the end of the month. For the man who is paid by the hour, that means never saying no to overtime. For the man whose loyalty to the organization is measured in time at his desk, it means goodbye to nine to five.

5   To lots of small children it means a visiting father. The standard joke in one large corporate office is that the dads always say their children look like angels when they're sleeping because that's the only way they ever see them. A Gallup survey taken several years ago showed that roughly 12 percent of the men surveyed with children under the age of six worked more than sixty hours a week, and an additional 25 percent worked between fifty and sixty hours. (Less than 8 percent of the working women surveyed who had children of that age worked those hours.)

6   No matter how you divide it up, those are twelve-hour days. When talk-show host Jane Wallace adopted a baby recently, she said one reason she was not troubled by becoming a mother without becoming a wife was that many of her married female friends were "functionally single," given the hours their husbands worked. The evening commuter rush is getting longer. The 7:45 to West BackofBeyond is more crowded than ever before. The eight o'clock dad. The nine o'clock dad.

7   There's a horribly sad irony to this, and it is that the quality of fathering is better than it was when the dads left work at five o'clock and came home to café curtains and tuna casserole. The five o'clock dad was remote,

a "Wait till your father gets home" kind of dad with a newspaper for a face. The roles he and his wife had were clear: she did nurture and home, he did discipline and money. The role fathers have carved out for themselves today is a vast improvement, a muddling of those old boundaries. Those of us obliged to convert behavior into trends have probably been a little heavy-handed on the shared childbirth and egalitarian diaper-changing. But fathers today do seem to be more emotional with their children, more nurturing, more open. Many say, "My father never told me he loved me," and so they tell their own children all the time that they love them.

8   When they're home.

9   There are people who think that this is changing even as we speak, that there is a kind of perestroika* of home and work that we will look on as beginning at the beginning of the 1990s. A nonprofit organization called the Families and Work Institute advises corporations on how to balance personal and professional obligations and concerns, and Ellen Galinsky, its co-founder, says she has noticed a change in the last year.

10   "When we first started doing this the groups of men and of women sounded very different," she said. "If the men complained at all about long hours, they complained about their wives' complaints. Now if the timbre of the voice was disguised I couldn't tell which is which. The men are saying: 'I don't want to live this way anymore. I want to be with my kids.' I think the corporate culture will have to begin to respond to that."

11   This change can only be to the good, not only for women but especially for men, and for kids, too. The stereotypical five o'clock dad belongs in a diorama, with his "Ask your mother" and his "Don't be a crybaby." The father who believes hugs and kisses are sex-blind and a dirty diaper requires a change, not a woman, is infinitely preferable. What a joy it would be if he were around more.

---

* perestroika – a Russian term for restructuring

1 Where would you most likely find this essay?

A. an encyclopedia

B. a history book

C. a magazine

D. a science journal

Ⓐ Ⓑ Ⓒ Ⓓ

SIDEBAR INSTRUCTION
Think about what the author is saying in this essay. What writing style does she use? Then think about the types of literature in the answer choices. Which one is the best match?

2 Essays include many different elements of writing. Which of the following best describes the writing in this selection?

A. plot

B. characterization

C. dialogue

D. conflict

Ⓐ Ⓑ Ⓒ Ⓓ

SIDEBAR INSTRUCTION
Every type of writing, including essays, involves several elements. Think about each of your answer choices and decide which element is the one primarily used in this selection.

3 What was the author's purpose in writing this essay?

A. to encourage women to be angry with men

B. to examine a troubling aspect of our society

C. to suggest that men and women trade lifestyles

D. to advise men to leave their jobs

Ⓐ Ⓑ Ⓒ Ⓓ

SIDEBAR INSTRUCTION
Every good essay needs a purpose or a reason. Why did the author write this essay? Think about the points she made in the selection. What is her primary purpose?

4 Which is an example of factual evidence that supports the author's point of view?

A. The quality of fathering is better than it was when the dads left work at five o'clock and came home to café curtains and tuna casserole.

B. Fathers today do seem to be more emotional with their children, more nurturing, more open.

C. A nonprofit organization called the Families and Work Institute advises corporations on how to balance personal and professional obligations.

D. The stereotypical five o'clock dad belongs in a diorama.

Ⓐ   Ⓑ   Ⓒ   Ⓓ

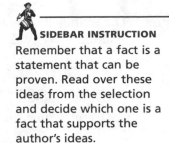

SIDEBAR INSTRUCTION
Remember that a fact is a statement that can be proven. Read over these ideas from the selection and decide which one is a fact that supports the author's ideas.

5 Which is one device the author uses in her essay?

A. interviews

B. examples

C. compare and contrast

D. autobiographical information

Ⓐ   Ⓑ   Ⓒ   Ⓓ

SIDEBAR INSTRUCTION
As in any type of writing, essays can include many kinds of devices. Think about each of these and decide which one was used in the essay.

6 The author includes a quote from Ellen Galinsky, co-founder of the Families and Work Institute. What is her purpose in doing this?

A. to show that men's feelings are changing

B. to explain that men and women both work long hours

C. to convince the reader that men should work fewer hours

D to describe what it is like to raise children in today's society

Ⓐ   Ⓑ   Ⓒ   Ⓓ

SIDEBAR INSTRUCTION
Reread Ellen Galinsky's quote. What message does it convey?

101

7   The author begins this essay with a statement she overheard in a restaurant. Why does she do this?

A. to use a unique writing device

B. to include quotes within her essay

C. to introduce the main idea of her essay

D. to state her position on the issue discussed in the essay

Ⓐ   Ⓑ   Ⓒ   Ⓓ

SIDEBAR INSTRUCTION
Reread the opening statement. Think about the main idea of the essay. Is the main idea stated in this quote?

8   Why does the author of "Men at Work" believe today's fathers are better than the fathers of the past? Support your answer with details and information from the essay.

_____

_____

_____

_____

_____

_____

_____

_____

_____

_____

STEP THREE ON YOUR OWN

Read the passage. Then answer the questions that follow.

from
I Stand Here Ironing

by Tillie Olsen

1   I stand here ironing, and what you asked me moves tormented back and forth with the iron.

2   "I wish you would manage the time to come in and talk with me about your daughter. I'm sure you can help me understand her. She's a youngster who needs help and who I'm deeply interested in helping."

3   "Who needs help."…Even if I came, what good would it do? You think because I am her mother I have a key, or that in some way you could use me as a key? She has lived for nineteen years. There is all that life that has happened outside of me, beyond me. . . .

4   She was a beautiful baby. She blew shining bubbles of sound. She loved motion, loved light, loved color and music and textures. . . . She was a miracle to me, but when she was eight months old I had to leave her daytimes with the woman downstairs to whom she was no miracle at all. . . .

5   I was nineteen. It was the pre-relief, pre-WPA* world of the depression. I would start running as soon as I got off the streetcar, running up the stairs, the place smelling sour, and awake or asleep to startle awake, and when she saw me she would break into a clogged weeping that could not be comforted, a weeping I can hear yet.

6   After a while I found a job hashing* at night so I could be with her days, and it was better. But it came to where I had to bring her to [her father's] family and leave her.

7   It took a long time to raise the money for her fare back. . . . When she finally came, I hardly knew her, walking quick and nervous like her father, looking like her father, thin, and dressed in a shoddy red that yellowed her skin . . . . All the baby loveliness gone.

8   She was two. Old enough for nursery school … She always had a reason why wc should stay home. Momma, you look sick, Momma. I feel sick. Momma, the teachers aren't there today, they're sick. Momma, we can't go, there was a fire last night. Momma, it's a holiday today, no school, they told me.

9   But never a direct protest, never rebellion. I think of others in their three-, four-year-oldness—the explosions, the tempers, the denunciations, the demands—and I feel suddenly ill. I put the iron down. What in me demanded that goodness in her? And what was the cost, the cost of such goodness?

10   The old man living in the back once said in his gentle way: "You should smile at Emily more when you look at her." What was in my face when I looked at her? I loved her. There were all the acts of love.

11   It was only with the others that I remembered what he said, and it was the face of joy, and not of care or tightness or worry I turned to them—too late for Emily. She does not smile easily, let alone almost always as her bothers and sisters do. . . .

12   She did not get well. She stayed skeleton thin, not wanting to eat, and night after night she had nightmares. She would call for me, and I would rouse from exhaustion to sleepily call back, "You're all right, darling, go to sleep, it's just a dream," and if she still called, in a sterner voice, "now go to sleep, Emily, there's nothing to hurt you." Twice, only twice, when I had to get up for Susan anyhow, I went to sit with her.

13   Now when it is too late (as if she would let me hold and comfort her like I do the others) I get up and go to her at once at her moan or restless stirring. "Are you awake, Emily? Can I get you something?" And the answer is always the same: "No, I'm all right, go back to sleep, Mother." . . .

14   She is coming. She runs up the stairs two at a time with her light graceful step, and I know she is happy tonight. Whatever it was that occasioned your call did not happen today.

15   "Aren't you ever going to finish the ironing, Mother? Whistler painted his mother in a rocker. I'd have to paint mine standing over an ironing board." This is one of her communicative nights where she tells me everything as she fixes herself a plate of food out of the icebox.

16   She is so lovely. Why did you want me to come in at all? Why were you concerned? She will find her way. . . . Only help her to know—help make it so there is cause for her to know—that she is more than this dress on the ironing board, helpless before the iron.

---

* WPA – Works Progress Administration, a government agency founded in 1935 to provide work for unemployed Americans suffering through the Great Depression.

* hashing – working in a cheap restaurant

9 What type, or genre, of writing is this selection?

A. fiction

B. science fiction

C. biography

D. myth

Ⓐ Ⓑ Ⓒ Ⓓ

10 What was the author's purpose in writing this passage?

A. to tell the reader about her own experiences as a young single mother

B. to explain her theory on how children are like ironed clothing

C. to describe how a mother's struggles cause her daughter to suffer

D. to help mothers improve their relationships with their daughters

Ⓐ Ⓑ Ⓒ Ⓓ

11 The author of this selection writes in which point-of-view?

A. first person

B. second person

C. third person

D. omniscient

Ⓐ Ⓑ Ⓒ Ⓓ

12 Stories include many different elements of writing. Which of the following **best** describes the writing in this selection?

A. dialogue

B. characterization

C. description

D. interview

Ⓐ Ⓑ Ⓒ Ⓓ

13 The author refers to one of Emily's "communicative nights." What is her purpose in doing this?

A. to explain that Emily does not need help from her teacher

B. to reassure parents that their children will find their own ways in life

C. to defend herself from the possible criticisms of Emily's teacher

D. to show that the hardships of Emily's childhood have not ruined her

Ⓐ Ⓑ Ⓒ Ⓓ

14 Write a character sketch on the daughter from "I Stand here Ironing"
using details and information from this selection.

_____

_____

_____

_____

_____

_____

_____

_____

_____

_____

LESSON 6

Students will identify, analyze, and apply knowledge of theme in literature and provide evidence from the text to support their understanding.

WHAT THIS STANDARD MEANS

Questions assessing this standard will ask you about the theme of a piece of literature. Remember that the theme is the central idea or the message the author is trying to convey. It is not stated in the passage. It is the underlying meaning of the passage. The theme represents a view or comment on life.

STEP ONE   TEN-MINUTE LESSON

Sample Passage

Excerpt from

Of Mice and Men

by John Steinbeck

1   A few miles south of Soledad, the Salinas River drops in close to the hillside bank and runs deep and green. The water is warm too, for it has slipped twinkling over the yellow sands in the sunlight before reaching the narrow pool. On one side of the river the golden foothill slopes curve up to the strong and rocky Gabilan mountains, but on the valley side the water is lined with trees— willows fresh and green with every spring, carrying in their lower leaf junctures the debris of the winter's flooding; and sycamores with mottled, white, recumbent limbs and branches that arch over the pool. On the sandy bank under the trees the leaves lie deep and so crisp that a lizard makes a great skittering if he runs among them. Rabbits come out of the brush to sit on the sand in the evening, and the damp flats are covered with the night tracks of 'coons, and with the spread pads of dogs from the ranches, and with the split-wedge tracks of deer that come to drink in the dark.

2   There is a path through the willows and among the sycamores, a path beaten hard by boys coming down from the ranches to swim in the deep pool, and beaten hard by tramps who come wearily down from the highway in the evening to jungle-up near water. In front of the low horizontal limb of a giant sycamore there is an ash pile made by many fires; the limb is worn smooth by men who have sat on it.

Sample Questions

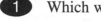 Which word best describes the scene in the passage?

A. mundane

B. mysterious

C. exhilarating

D. enchanting

Ⓐ   Ⓑ   Ⓒ   Ⓓ

Answer choice A: *Mundane* means "boring." The place the author is describing seems peaceful; but not boring. This is not the correct answer choice.

Answer choice B: The place the author is describing might be mysterious since it certainly is not a common sight. However, there is probably a better answer choice.

Answer choice C: *Exhilarating* means "exciting." The author obviously likes the place he is describing, but he is probably not trying to convey that it is exhilarating.

Answer choice D: The place the author is describing is definitely enchanting. *Enchanting* means "charming." This is the correct answer choice.

2 In this passage, the author is describing a place. What would be an appropriate title for this excerpt based on its theme? Explain why the title you choose is appropriate. Use relevant and specific details from the excerpt in your answer.

_____

_____

_____

_____

_____

_____

_____

_____

_____

_____

This question asks you to choose a title reflecting the theme of the excerpt. Reread the excerpt. What kind of impression do the author's words make? Consider the second paragraph. Why is there a path leading to the water? You might want to choose a title such as "A Path to Peace" or "A Tranquil Hideaway." Use details from the excerpt to explain why your title is an appropriate title.

3 What is the tone of this passage?

A. reflective

B. tranquil

C. objective

D. sentimental

Ⓐ   Ⓑ   Ⓒ   Ⓓ

Answer choice A: This question asks you to identify the tone of this passage. The answer choice, *reflective*, implies that someone is reminiscing about the past. The passage is mostly descriptive, so this is probably not the best answer choice.

Answer choice B: The word *tranquil* means "peaceful." This is a good answer choice, but you should always consider each answer choice before making a final decision.

Answer choice C: When the tone of a passage is objective, the author reports what he or she sees without indicating any feelings about the subject. The author of this passage obviously likes the place he is describing, so this is not the best answer choice.

Answer choice D: Something that is sentimental is very emotional. While the author conveys some emotion in this passage, it is mostly descriptive and describes a peaceful setting. Answer choice B is the best answer choice.

STEP TWO SIDEBAR INSTRUCTION

Read the passage and answer the questions that follow. Use the Sidebar Instruction to help you choose the best answer.

A Conversation with My Father

by Grace Paley

1   My father is eighty-six years old and in bed. His heart, that bloody motor, is equally old and will not do certain jobs any more. It still floods his head with brainy light. But it won't let his legs carry the weight of his body around the house. Despite my metaphors, this muscle failure is not due to his old heart, he says, but to a potassium shortage. Sitting on one pillow, leaning on three, he offers last-minute advice and makes a request.

2   "I would like you to write a simple story just once more," he says, "the kind de Maupassant wrote, or Chekhov, the kind you used to write. Just recognizable people and then write down what happened to them next."

3   I say, "Yes, why not? That's possible." I want to please him, though I don't remember writing that way. I would like to try to tell such a story, if he means the kind that begins: "There was a woman . . ." followed by plot, the absolute line between two points which I've always despised. Not for literary reasons, but because it takes all hope away.

Everyone, real or invented, deserves the open destiny of life.

4   Finally I thought of a story that had been happening for a couple of years right across the street. I wrote it down, then read it aloud. "Pa," I said, "how about this? Do you mean something like this?"

5   Once in my time there was a woman and she had a son. They lived nicely, in a small apartment in Manhattan. This boy at about fifteen became a junkie, which is not unusual in our neighborhood. In order to maintain her close friendship with him, she became a junkie, too. She said it was part of the youth culture, with which she felt very much at home. After a while, for a number of reasons, the boy gave it all up and left the city and his mother in disgust. Hopeless and alone, she grieved. We all visit her.

6   "O.K., Pa, that's it," I said, "an unadorned and miserable tale."

7   "But that's not what I mean," my father said. "You misunderstand me on purpose. You know there's a lot more to it. You know that. You left everything out. Turgenev

wouldn't do that. Chekhov wouldn't do that. There are in fact Russian writers you never heard of, you don't have an inkling of, as good as anyone, who can write a plain ordinary story, who would not leave out what you have left out. I object not to facts but to people sitting in trees talking senselessly, voices from who knows where . . ."

8   "Forget that one, Pa, what have I left out now? In this one?"

9   "Her looks for instance."

10   "Oh. Quite handsome, I think. Yes."

11   "Her hair?"

12   "Dark, with heavy braids, as though she were a girl or a foreigner."

13   "What were her parents like, her stock? That she became such a person. It's interesting, you know."

14   "From out of town. Professional people. The first to be divorced in their county. How's that? Enough?" I asked.

15   "With you, it's all a joke," he said. "What about the boy's father? Why didn't you mention him? Who was he? Or was the boy born out of wedlock?"

16   "Yes," I said. "He was born out of wedlock."

17   "For Godsakes, doesn't anyone in your stories get married? . . . ."

18   "No," I said. "In real life, yes. But in my stories, no."

19   "Why do you answer me like that?"

20   "Oh, Pa, this is a simple story about a smart woman who came to N.Y.C. full of interest love trust excitement very up to date, and about her son, what a hard time she had in this world. Married or not, it's of small consequence."

21   "It's of great consequence," he said.

22   "O.K.," I said.

23   "O.K. O.K. yourself," he said, "but listen. I believe you that she's good-looking, but I don't think she was so smart."

24   "That's true," I said. "Actually that's the trouble with stories. People start out fantastic. You think they're extraordinary, but it turns out as the work goes along, they're just average with a good education. Sometimes the other way around, the person's a kind of dumb innocent, but he outwits you and you can't even think of an ending good enough."

25   "What do you do then?" he asked. He had been a doctor for a couple of decades and then an artist for a couple of decades and he's still interested in details, crafts, technique.

26   "Well, you just have to let the story lie around till some agreement can be reached between you and the stubborn hero."

27   "Aren't you talking silly now?" he asked. "Start again," he said. "It so happens I'm not going out this evening. Tell the story again. See what you can do this time."

1 What is the main reason the narrator and her father cannot agree?

A. He is a more talented writer than her.

B. They view life differently because of their ages.

C. They like to watch different television programs.

D. She thinks most people have average intelligence.

Ⓐ Ⓑ Ⓒ Ⓓ

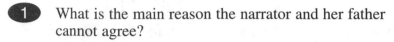**SIDEBAR INSTRUCTION**
Think about the major conflict between the father and the daughter. Why are they having this conflict? What kind of story does he want her to write?

2 What motivates the daughter to write the kind of story her father asks her to write?

A. She wants to make him happy.

B. She knows he has great knowledge.

C. She hopes to learn to write in a new way.

D. She is aware that her father is usually right.

Ⓐ Ⓑ Ⓒ Ⓓ

SIDEBAR INSTRUCTION
This question asks you to identify the daughter's motivation. What condition is her father in? Why does she try to do as he asks?

3 What does the narrator's father dislike about her stories?

A. They are about people she knows from her neighborhood.

B. They leave out important basic details of the characters' lives.

C. They are about good looking unintelligent people.

D. They contain believable characters that do nothing extraordinary.

Ⓐ Ⓑ Ⓒ Ⓓ

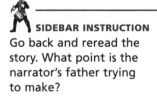**SIDEBAR INSTRUCTION**
Go back and reread the story. What point is the narrator's father trying to make?

4 How does the father feel about his daughter's responses to questions?

A. intrigued

B. hopeful

C. frustrated

D. suspicious

Ⓐ   Ⓑ   Ⓒ   Ⓓ

> **SIDEBAR INSTRUCTION**
> Reread the dialogue between the father and his daughter.

5 What is the theme of this story? Use relevant and specific information from the story to support your answer.

_____

_____

_____

_____

_____

> **SIDEBAR INSTRUCTION**
> Think about why the author wrote this story. What message is she trying to convey?

6 When the narrator tells her father that it is of little consequence whether the characters in her stories are married, her father replies: It is of great consequence." How does this sentence relate to the theme of the story?

_____

_____

_____

_____

_____

> **SIDEBAR INSTRUCTION**
> Think about the way the father feels about his daughter's stories. What is he trying to teach her?

STEP THREE **ON YOUR OWN**

Read the following poems by Emily Dickinson and answer the questions that follow.

Because I could not stop for Death

1   Because I could not stop for Death—
    He kindly stopped for me—
    The Carriage held but just Ourselves—
    And Immortality.

5   We slowly drove—He knew no haste
    And I had put away
    My labor and my leisure too,
    For His Civility—

    We passed the School, where Children strove
10 At Recess—in the Ring—
    We passed the Fields of Gazing Grain—
    We passed the Setting Sun—

    Or rather—He passed Us—
    The Dews drew quivering and chill—
15 For only Gossamer, my Gown—
    My Tippet[1]—only Tulle[2]—

    We paused before a House that seemed
    A Swelling of the Ground—
    The Roof was scarcely visible—
20 The Cornice—in the Ground—

    Since then—'tis Centuries—and yet
    Feels shorter than the Day
    I first surmised the Horses' Heads
    Were toward Eternity—

---

[1] Tippet: shawl
[2] Tulle: a net made of silk

I heard a Fly buzz— when I died

1   I heard a Fly buzz—when I died—
The Stillness in the Room
Was like the Stillness in the Air—
Between the Heaves of Storm—

5   The Eyes around—had wrung them dry—
And Breaths were gathering firm
For the last Onset—when the King
Be witnessed—in the Room—

I will my Keepsakes—Signed Away
10   What portion of me be
Assignable—and then it was
There interposed a Fly—

With Blue—uncertain stumbling Buzz—
Between the light—and me—
15 And then the Windows failed—and then
I could not see to see—

7 How does the speaker in "Because I could not stop for Death" view death?

A. as a house swelling from the ground

B. as a gentleman driving a carriage

C. as a man who is in a hurry to take her somewhere

D. as a peaceful sunset over a field

Ⓐ Ⓑ Ⓒ Ⓓ

8 Which word best describes the atmosphere in "I heard a Fly buzz— when I died"?

A. rushed

B. peaceful

C. anxious

D. turmoil

Ⓐ Ⓑ Ⓒ Ⓓ

9 Which word best personifies Death in "Because I could not stop for Death"?

A. repulsive

B. frightening

C. mannerly

D. indifferent

Ⓐ Ⓑ Ⓒ Ⓓ

10 Which word best describes the narrator of "I heard a Fly buzz—when I died"?

A. anxious

B. perceptive

C. regretful

D. mysterious

Ⓐ Ⓑ Ⓒ Ⓓ

11 How are the themes of these two poems alike? Use relevant and specific information from both poems in your answer.

_____

_____

_____

_____

_____

_____

_____

_____

This section reviews the standards you have just learned. The questions in this review are for Standards 9, 10, and 11.

The Story of an Hour

by Kate Chopin

1   Knowing that Mrs. Mallard was afflicted with heart trouble, great care was taken to break to her as gently as possible the news of her husband's death.

2   It was her sister Josephine who told her, in broken sentences, veiled hints that revealed in half concealing. Her husband's friend Richards was there, too, near her. It was he who had been in the newspaper office when intelligence of the railroad disaster was received, with Brently Mallard's name leading the list of "killed." He had only taken the time to assure himself of its truth by a second telegram, and had hastened to forestall any less careful, less tender friend in bearing the sad message.

3   She did not hear the story as many women have heard the same, with a paralyzed inability to accept its significance. She wept at once, with sudden, wild abandonment, in her sister's arms. When the storm of grief had spent itself she went away to her room alone. She would have no one follow her.

4   There stood, facing the open window, a comfortable, roomy armchair. Into this she sank, pressed down by a physical exhaustion that haunted her body and seemed to reach into her soul.

5   She could see in the open square before her house the tops of trees that were all aquiver with the new spring life. The delicious breath of rain was in the air. In the street below a peddler was crying his wares. The notes of a distant song which someone was singing reached her family and countless sparrows were twittering in the eaves.

6   There were patches of blue sky showing here and there through the clouds that had met and piled above the other in the west facing her window.

7   She sat with her head thrown back upon the cushion of the chair quite motionless, except when a sob came up into her throat and shook her, as a child who has cried itself to sleep continues to sob in its dreams.

8   She was young, with a fair, calm face, whose lines bespoke repression and even a certain strength. But now there was a dull stare in her eyes, whose gaze was fixed away off yonder on one of those patches of blue sky. It was not a glance of reflection, but rather indicated a suspension of intelligent thought.

9   There was something coming to her and she was waiting for it, fearfully. What was it? She did not know; it was too subtle and elusive to name. But she felt it, creeping out of the sky, reaching toward her through the sounds, the scents, the color that filled the air.

10   Now her bosom rose and fell tumultuously. She was beginning to recognize this thing that was approaching to possess her, and she was striving to beat it back with her will—as powerless as her two white slender hands would have been.

11   When she abandoned herself a little whispered word escaped her slightly parted lips. She said it over and over under her breath: "Free, free, free!" The vacant stare and the look of terror that had followed it went from her eyes. They stayed keen and bright. Her pulses beat fast, and the coursing blood warmed and relaxed every inch of her body.

12   She did not stop to ask if it were not a monstrous joy that held her. A clear and exalted perception enabled her to dismiss the suggestion as trivial.

13   She knew that she would weep again when she saw the kind, tender hands folded in death; the face that had never looked save with love upon her, fixed and gray and dead. But she saw beyond that bitter moment a long procession of years to come that would belong to her absolutely. And she opened and spread her arms out to them in welcome.

14   There would be no one to live for her during those coming years; she would live for herself. There would be no powerful will bending her in that blind persistence with which men and women believe they have a right to impose a private will upon a fellow creature. A kind intention or a cruel intention made the act seem no less a crime as she looked upon it in that brief moment of illumination.

15   And yet she had loved him—sometimes. Often she had not. What did it matter! What could love, the unsolved mystery, count for in face of this possession of self-assertion which she suddenly recognized as the strongest impulse of her being.

16   "Free! Body and soul free!" she kept whispering.

120

17   Josephine was kneeling before the closed door with her lips to the keyhole, imploring for admission. "Louise, open the door! I beg; open the door—you will make yourself ill. What are you doing, Louise? For heaven's sake open the door."

18   "Go away. I am not making myself ill." No; she was drinking in a very elixir of life through that open window.

19   Her fancy was running riot along those days ahead of her. Spring days, summer days, and all sorts of days that would be her own. She breathed a quick prayer that life might be long. It was only yesterday she had thought with a shudder that life might be long.

20   She arose at length and opened the door to her sister's importunities. There was a feverish triumph in her eyes, and she carried herself unwittingly like a goddess of Victory. She clasped her sister's waist, and together they descended the stairs. Richards stood waiting for them at the bottom.

21   Some one was opening the front door with a latchkey. It was Brently Mallard who entered, a little travel-stained, composedly carrying his gripsack and umbrella. He had been far from the scene of accident, and did not even know there had been one. He stood amazed at Josephine's piercing cry; at Richards' quick motion to screen him from the view of his wife.

22   But Richards was too late.

23   When the doctors came they said she had died of heart disease—of joy that kills.

1 How does Mrs. Mallard feel about her husband's death?

A. She is shocked at first, but then happy.

B. She is deeply saddened and confused.

C. She is sad at first, but then terrified.

D. She is relieved at first, but then saddened.

Ⓐ Ⓑ Ⓒ Ⓓ

2 Which point of view does the author use in this selection?

A. first person

B. second person

C. third person

D. editorial omniscient

Ⓐ Ⓑ Ⓒ Ⓓ

3 Which literary device is used by the author in this passage?

A. sarcasm

B. irony

C. flashback

D. alliteration

Ⓐ Ⓑ Ⓒ Ⓓ .

4 How does Richards learn of Brently Mallard's death?

A. He receives a telegram from a concerned friend.

B. He sees it on a list of people killed in an accident.

C. He reads about it in the newspaper.

D. He is told about it from a peddler on the street.

Ⓐ Ⓑ Ⓒ Ⓓ

5 Which word best describes how Louise feels about being married?

A. content

B. ecstatic

C. nostalgic

D. confined

Ⓐ Ⓑ Ⓒ Ⓓ

6 What does Louise plan to do in the days ahead?

A. fondly remember the past

B. live her life to the fullest

C. come to terms with her grief

D. spend time with family and friends

Ⓐ Ⓑ Ⓒ Ⓓ

7 What is the theme of this story? Use relevant details and information
from the story in your answer.

_____

_____

_____

_____

_____

_____

_____

_____

_____

LESSON 7

Students will identify, analyze, and apply knowledge of the structure and elements of fiction and provide evidence from the text to support their understanding.

WHAT THIS STANDARD MEANS

Questions assessed by this benchmark will ask you about elements of fiction. You might be asked to analyze parts of a story to determine an author's meaning. You might also be asked to draw a conclusion about characters in the story. You may also be asked to identify elements of fiction, such as irony, foreshadowing, point of view, and symbolism.

125

STEP ONE **TEN-MINUTE LESSON**

Sample Passage

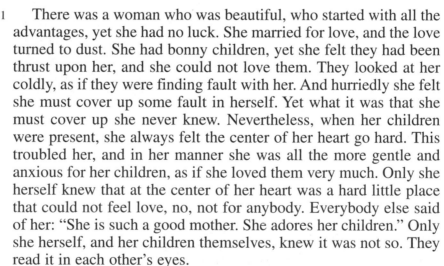

from
The Rocking-Horse Winner
by D.H. Lawrence

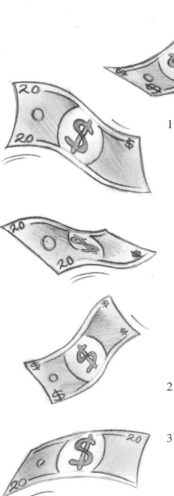

1   There was a woman who was beautiful, who started with all the advantages, yet she had no luck. She married for love, and the love turned to dust. She had bonny children, yet she felt they had been thrust upon her, and she could not love them. They looked at her coldly, as if they were finding fault with her. And hurriedly she felt she must cover up some fault in herself. Yet what it was that she must cover up she never knew. Nevertheless, when her children were present, she always felt the center of her heart go hard. This troubled her, and in her manner she was all the more gentle and anxious for her children, as if she loved them very much. Only she herself knew that at the center of her heart was a hard little place that could not feel love, no, not for anybody. Everybody else said of her: "She is such a good mother. She adores her children." Only she herself, and her children themselves, knew it was not so. They read it in each other's eyes.

2   There were a boy and two little girls. They lived in a pleasant house, with a garden, and they had discreet servants, and felt themselves superior to anyone in the neighborhood.

3   Although they lived in style, they felt always an anxiety in the house. There was never enough money. The mother had a small income, and the father had a small income, but not nearly enough for the social position which they had to keep up. The father went into town to some office. But though he had good prospects, these prospects never materialized. There was always the grinding sense of the shortage of money, though the style was always kept up.

Sample Questions

1 According to the excerpt, why doesn't the woman love her children?

A. She was not capable of feeling love for anybody.

B. She never wanted to have children.

C. She hated her husband.

D. She was afraid of losing her social status.

(A)　(B)　(C)　(D)

This question asks you to look at the character of the mother in this selection. The story gives a lot of information about her and the way she feels about her life. To answer this question, focus on the mother's inability to love her children. What does the author imply regarding the mother's feelings towards her children?

Answer choice A: Think about what the author says about the woman's capacity to love anybody. She wants to love her children yet "she knew at the center of her heart was a hard place that could not feel love, no not for anybody." Because she is incapable of loving anybody, her children unfortunately are included. This appears to be the correct answer, but read the other choices just to make sure.

Answer choice B: Think about what the author told us about the woman. He wrote that she felt the children "had been thrust upon her." She didn't want the responsibility of motherhood and could not love the children. Yet, we do not know if she ever wanted to have children. This is not the correct answer choice.

Answer choice C: Does the woman treat the children coldly because she hates her husband? The woman's husband is mentioned in the story, though just briefly. He doesn't seem very involved in the story, and there is no mention of her hating him. This is not the correct answer choice.

Answer choice D: Did the woman emotionally neglect her children to help her social status? She is concerned about her social status, but the story tells us that people were always impressed with her because they thought she loved her children. Not loving her children would have actually hurt her social status, so this is not the correct answer. The best answer choice is A.

2 What does the author mean when he writes that the father "had good prospects" but "these prospects never materialized"?

A. The father meant well but always made mistakes.

B. The family pretended to support the father but never did.

C The father had many ideas about the world, but they were incorrect.

D. The father had good job opportunities but never had good jobs.

This question asks you to interpret one of the phrases the author uses in the story to describe the father. You can look back to the story in order to find this phrase in its context. Carefully read the answer choices and decide which one defines the phrase. Think about the meaning of the word *prospects*. What are good prospects, and what is happening if good prospects don't materialize?

Answer choice A: Is the author saying that the father tried to do his best but ended up making things worse? This may be the case, as the family seems very unlucky, but this is not directly expressed in the story. This may be the correct answer choice, but you should read the other answers to make sure.

Answer choice B: Think about the meaning of the word *prospects*. Family members aren't included in this definition of prospects. Whether or not the family truly supported the father is not clearly stated. You can eliminate this answer choice.

Answer choice C: Did the father have many incorrect ideas about the world? It sounds as if he may have because he did not do very well. However, the phrase about the father's "good prospects" did not seem to refer to ideas. A prospect is usually more concrete than just an idea. There is probably a better answer choice.

Answer choice D: Is a job opportunity an example of a prospect? If the father had good job opportunities, but never actually got those jobs, he would have had good prospects that never materialized. Some of the other answer choices presented possible correct answers, but answer choice D is clearly the best answer choice.

Read the excerpt from the story in the box below.

> There was always the grinding sense of
> the shortage of money, though the style
> was always kept up.

3 This excerpt is an example of

A. a flashback.

B. characterization.

C. foreshadowing.

D. symbolism.

(A) (B) (C) (D)

Answer choice A: A *flashback* is a shift to an earlier time. Although we do know that the father's prospects never materialized, there is not enough information given to assume that something happened in the past to precipitate the families' shortage of money. This is not the correct answer choice.

Answer choice B: *Characterization* is the way an author presents a character and his or her attributes. We get an idea from this excerpt that this family is living in a style well beyond their means of support. This is an example of characterization, but there may be a better answer.

Answer choice C: *Foreshadowing* is a technique of giving clues to upcoming events. Money seems to be an issue with this family. They obviously are living beyond their means. There seems to be a hint that the story will be dealing with the financial woes of the family. There is always anxiety in the house. This seems to be the correct answer choice.

Answer choice D: *Symbolism* is using one thing to represent another thing. There is no symbolism in this excerpt; therefore, this is not the correct answer. The correct answer choice is C.

STEP TWO SIDEBAR INSTRUCTION

Read the selection and answer the questions that follow. Use the Sidebar Instruction to help you choose the correct answer.

Good Country People

by Flannery O'Connor

1   Besides the neutral expression that she wore when she was alone, Mrs. Freeman had two others, forward and reverse, that she used for all her human dealings. Her forward expression was steady and driving like the advance of a heavy truck. Her eyes never swerved to left or right but turned as the story turned as if they followed a yellow line down the center of it. She seldom used the other expression because it was not often necessary for her to retract a statement, but when she did, her face came to a complete stop, there was an almost imperceptible movement of her black eyes, during which they seemed to be receding, and then the observer would see that Mrs. Freeman, though she might stand there as real as several grain sacks thrown on top of each other, was no longer there in spirit. As for getting anything across to her when this was the case, Mrs. Hopewell had given it up. She might talk her head off. Mrs. Freeman could never be brought to admit herself wrong on any point. She would stand there and if she could be brought to say anything, it was something like, "Well, I wouldn't of said it was and I wouldn't of said it wasn't," or letting her gaze range over the top kitchen shelf where there was an assortment of dusty bottles, she might remark, "I see you ain't ate many of them figs you put up last summer."

2   They carried on their most important business in the kitchen at breakfast. Every morning Mrs. Hopewell got up at seven o'clock and lit her gas heater and Joy's. Joy was her daughter, a large blonde girl who had an artificial leg. Mrs. Hopewell thought of her as a child though she was thirty-two years old and highly educated. Joy would get up while her mother was eating and lumber into the bathroom and slam the door, and before long, Mrs. Freeman would arrive at the back door. Joy would hear her mother call, "Come on in," and then would talk for a while in low voices that were indistinguishable in the bathroom. By the

130

time Joy came in, they had usually finished the weather report and were on one or the other of Mrs. Freeman's daughters, Glynese or Carramae. Joy called them Glycerin and Caramel. Glynese, a red head, was eighteen and had many admirers; Carramae, a blonde, was only fifteen but already married and pregnant. She could not keep anything in her stomach. Every morning Mrs. Freeman told Mrs. Hopewell how many times she had vomited since the last report.

3   Mrs. Hopewell liked to tell people that Glynese and Carramae were two of the finest girls she knew and that Mrs. Freeman was a *lady* and that she was never ashamed to take her anywhere or introduce her to anybody they might meet. Then she would tell how she happened to hire the Freemans in the first place and how they were a godsend to her and how she had them four years. The reason for her keeping them so long was that they were not trash. They were good country people. She had telephoned the man whose name they had given as a reference and he had told her that Mr. Freeman was a good farmer but that his wife was the noisiest woman to walk the earth. "She's got to be into everything," the man said. "If she don't get there before the dust settles, you can bet she's dead, that's all. She'll want to know all your business. I can stand him real good," he had said, "but me nor my wife neither could

have stood that woman one more minute on this place." That had put Mrs. Hopewell off for a few days.

4   She had hired them in the end because there were no other applicants but she had made up her mind beforehand exactly how she would handle the woman. Since she was the type who had to be into everything, then, Mrs. Hopewell had decided, she would not only let her be into everything, she would *see to it* that she was into everything—she would give her the responsibility of everything, she would put her in charge. Mrs. Hopewell had no bad qualities of her own but she was able to use other people's in such a constructive way that she never felt the lack. She had hired the Freemans and she had kept them for four years.

5   Nothing is perfect. This was one of Mrs. Hopewell's favorite sayings. Another was: that is life! And still another, and most important, was: well, other people have their opinions too. She would make these statements, usually at the table, in a tone of gentle insistence as if no one held them but her, and the large hulking Joy, whose constant outrage had obliterated every expression from her face, would stare just a little to the side of her, her eyes icy blue, with the look of someone who has achieved blindness by an act of will and means to keep it.

1 Mrs. Hopewell's daughter is named Joy. Based on information in this story, her name is

A. symbolic.

B. ironic.

C. persuasive.

D. exclamatory.

Ⓐ Ⓑ Ⓒ Ⓓ

SIDEBAR INSTRUCTION
Think about the way Joy acts in the selection. Does her behavior indicate any kind of joyfulness? Why did the author likely select that name for her?

2 According to the selection, what is Carramae's problem?

A. She is a gossip.

B. She has morning sickness.

C. She has an artificial leg.

D. She is constantly angry.

Ⓐ Ⓑ Ⓒ Ⓓ

SIDEBAR INSTRUCTION
This story mentions several characters, each of whom has problems. Think about the character Carramae, and what is said about her during the story. If you don't remember, look back.

Read the excerpt from the story in the box below.

> She's got to be the noisiest woman to walk the earth . . . If she don't get there before the dust settles, you can bet she's dead.

SIDEBAR INSTRUCTION
Think about what the man is saying about Mrs. Freeman. How may this affect Mrs. Hopewell's opinion of Mrs. Freeman?

3 What element of fiction best describes the man's reference of Mrs. Freeman given to Mrs. Hopewell?

A. foreshadowing

B. irony

C. symbolism

D. characterization

Ⓐ Ⓑ Ⓒ Ⓓ

4 The author writes that Joy has "the look of someone who has achieved blindness by an act of will and means to keep it." What does this statement suggest about Joy?

A. She is visually impaired.

B. She is satisfied with herself.

C. She is ignorant.

D. She is stubborn.

Ⓐ Ⓑ Ⓒ Ⓓ

SIDEBAR INSTRUCTION
Think about this statement about Joy. Is the author being literal? If the statement is figurative, what would that say about Joy?

Read the excerpt from the story in the box below.

> . . . and then the observer would see that Mrs. Freeman, though she might stand there as real as several grain sacks thrown on top of each other, was no longer there in spirit.

5 The author uses the image of "several grain sacks thrown on top of each other" to symbolize

A. physical presence.

B. emotional presence.

C. a great height.

D. a great weight.

Ⓐ Ⓑ Ⓒ Ⓓ

SIDEBAR INSTRUCTION
A symbol like grain sacks could mean several things. Think about what you've learned about Mrs. Freeman's attitude. Then read the excerpt carefully. What does this image symbolize?

6 The author conveys the mood by focusing on

A. the plot.

B. the setting.

C. the characters.

D. personification.

Ⓐ   Ⓑ   Ⓒ   Ⓓ

SIDEBAR INSTRUCTION
Eliminate answer choices that are obviously incorrect. Then consider which element of fiction conveys the mood.

7 Mrs. Hopewell has many different reactions to Mrs. Freeman in the excerpt. Identify one of these reactions and explain what it reveals about Mrs. Hopewell. Use relevant and specific information from the excerpt to support your answer.

_____

_____

_____

_____

_____

_____

_____

_____

_____

_____

STEP THREE **ON YOUR OWN**

Read the selection. Then answer the questions that follow.

from Night Before Battle

by Ernest Hemingway

1   At this time we were working in a shell-smashed house that overlooked the Casa del Campo in Madrid. Below us a battle was being fought. You could see it spread out below you and over the hills, could smell it, could taste the dust of it, and the noise of it was one great slithering sheet of rifle and automatic rifle fire rising and dropping, and in it came the crack of the guns and the bubbly rumbling of the outgoing shells fired from the batteries behind us, the thud of their bursts, and then the rolling yellow clouds of dust. But it was just too far to film well. We had tried working closer but they kept sniping at the camera and you could not work.

2   The big camera was the most expensive thing we had and if it was smashed we were through. We were making the film on almost nothing and all the money was in the cans of film and the cameras. We could not afford to waste film and you had to be awfully careful of the cameras.

3   The day before we had been sniped out of a good place to film from and I had to crawl back holding the small camera to my belly, trying to keep my head lower than my shoulders, hitching along on my elbows, the bullets whocking into the brick wall over my back and twice spurting dirt over me.

4   Our heaviest attacks were made in the afternoon, God knows why, as the fascists then had the sun at their backs, and it shone on the camera lenses and made them blink like a helio* and the Moors* would open up on the flash. They knew all about helios and officers' glasses from the Riff* and if you wanted to be properly sniped, all you had to do was use a pair of glasses without shading them adequately. They could shoot too, and they had kept my mouth dry all day.

5   In the afternoon we moved up into the house. It was a fine place to work and we made a sort of a blind for the camera on a balcony with the broken latticed curtains; but, as I said, it was too far.

6   It was not too far to get the pine studded hillside, the lake and the outline of the stone farm buildings that disappeared in the sudden smashes of stone dust from the hits by high explosive shells, nor was it too far to get the clouds of smoke and dirt that thundered up on the hill crest as the bombers droned over. But at eight hundred to a thousand yards the tanks looked like small mud-colored beetles bustling in the trees and spitting tiny flashes and the men behind them were toy men who lay flat, then crouched and ran, and then dropped to run again, or to stay where they lay, spotting the hillside as the tanks moved on. Still we hoped to get the shape of the battle. We had many close shots and would get others with luck and if we could get the sudden fountainings of earth, the puffs of shrapnel, the rolling clouds of smoke and dust lit by the yellow flash and white blossoming of grenades that is the very shape of battle we would have something that we needed.

---

*helio – here, a sun
*Moors – a group of people in Spain
*Riff – like the Moors, a group in Spain

8 What characteristic does the narrator possess?

A. laziness

B. determination

C. fear

D. pessimism

Ⓐ Ⓑ Ⓒ Ⓓ

9 In paragraph 2, what does the narrator mean when he writes that the cameramen "were making the film on almost nothing"?

A. They had obsolete equipment.

B. They had been unable to get any good footage.

C. They did not have a film subject in mind.

D. They had a very small budget.

Ⓐ Ⓑ Ⓒ Ⓓ

Read the sentence from the excerpt in the box below.

> They could shoot too, and they had kept my mouth dry all day.

10 What does the narrator mean by this statement?

A. The enemy kept the cameraman confined in the house.

B. The cameraman was running out of water.

C. The cameraman was nervous about being shot by the enemy.

D. The cameraman was overheated from the bright sun.

Ⓐ Ⓑ Ⓒ Ⓓ

11 From what point of view is this story written?

A. first person

B. second person

C. third person

D. omnescient narrator

Ⓐ Ⓑ Ⓒ Ⓓ

12 The narrator and his film crew face great danger in order to get footage of the battle. Identify **two** ways in which they put themselves at risk to continue their work, and explain what these risks reveal about the narrator. Use relevant and specific information from the excerpt to support your answer.

_____

_____

_____

_____

_____

_____

_____

_____

_____

_____

LESSON 8

Students will identify, analyze, and apply knowledge of the theme, structure, and elements of poetry and provide evidence from the text to support their understanding.

WHAT THIS STANDARD MEANS

Questions assessed by this standard will ask you about poetry. You might be asked to clarify the meaning of part of a poem or all of a poem. You might be asked to identify details or state the theme of a poem. You might be asked to analyze the effects of sound, form, figurative language, graphics and the dramatic structure of poetry.

STEP ONE TEN-MINUTE LESSON

Sample Passage

The Fly

by William Blake

1 Little Fly,
   Thy summer's play
   My thoughtless hand
4 Has brushed away.

   Am not I
   A fly like thee?
   Or art not thou
8 A man like me?

   For I dance
   And drink, and sing,
   Till some blind hand
12 Shall brush my wing.

   If thought is life
   And strength and breath
   And the want
16 Of thought is death;

   Then am I
   A happy fly,
   If I live,
20 Or if I die.

Sample Questions

1 What is the best word to describe the tone throughout this poem?

A. compassionate

B. reflective

C. sombre

D. comical

Ⓐ   Ⓑ   Ⓒ   Ⓓ

Answer choice A: The speaker's tone is somewhat compassionate since he seems upset that he carelessly brushed the fly away. However, there may be a better answer choice so be sure to read all answer choices.

Answer choice B: The speaker's tone is reflective. He thinks about how he and the fly are alike. He reflects on his mortality. This seems to be the best answer choice but read all answer choices.

Answer choice C: The speaker's tone is not sombre, so this is not the best answer choice.

Answer choice D: The tone of this poem is not humorous, so this is not the best answer choice. Answer choice B is the correct answer.

2 Which of the following figures of speech is used in lines 5–8?

A. simile

B. alliteration

C. analogy

D. onomatopoeia

Ⓐ   Ⓑ   Ⓒ   Ⓓ

Answer choice A: A *simile* is a comparison using *like* or *as*. There are no comparisons being made; therefore, this is not the correct answer choice.

Answer choice B: *Alliteration* is the repetition of consonant sounds. There is no repetition of consonant sounds in these lines, so this is not the correct answer choice.

Answer choice C: An *analogy* is a similarity between two things to show how they are alike. In lines 5–7 the author compares himself to a fly. This is the correct answer choice.

Answer choice D: *Onomatopoeia* is the use of words to make sounds which suggest their meaning, such as *hiss* and *purr*. There is not an example of onomatopoeia in these lines; therefore, this is not the correct answer choice.

3 What is the meaning of lines 9–12?

A. The speaker will have his wing brushed by a blind hand.

B. The speaker will enjoy life to its fullest until it is over.

C. A fly will brush away the speaker like the speaker brushed away the fly.

D. The speaker is a blind singer and dancer.

Ⓐ　Ⓑ　Ⓒ　Ⓓ

Answer choice A: In these lines, the speaker will literally be brushed away by some blind hand, but figuratively this is not what the lines mean. This is not the right answer choice.

Answer choice B: Figuratively, these lines mean that the speaker will enjoy life until it is over. Dancing, drinking, and singing represent living life to its fullest. The speaker's frivolity will cease once his wing is brushed by death. This is probably the correct answer, yet read all of the choices before making a decision.

Answer choice C: Literally the blind hand is a fly, but figuratively the fly could symbolize somebody or something else. This is not the correct answer choice.

Answer choice D: The speaker of this poem is not blind so this is not the correct answer choice. Answer choice B is the correct answer choice.

STEP TWO SIDEBAR INSTRUCTION

Read the poem and answer the questions that follow. Use the Sidebar Instruction to help you choose the correct answer.

Uphill

by Christina Rosetti (1830 – 1894)

1   Does the road wind uphill all the way?
      Yes, to the very end.
   Will the day's journey take the whole long day?
4   From morn to night, my friend.

   But is there for the night a resting-place?
      A roof for when the slow dark hours begin.
   May not the darkness hide it from my face?
8   You cannot miss that inn.

   Shall I meet other wayfarers at night?
      Those who have gone before.
   Then must I knock, or call when just in sight?
12   They will not keep you standing at the door.

   Shall I find comfort, travel-sore and weak?
      Of labor you shall find the sum.
   Will there be beds for me and all who seek?
16   Yea, beds for all who come.

1 In lines 3–4, what is analagous to "the whole long day"?

A. a lifetime

B. a night

C. a day

D. a week

Ⓐ Ⓑ Ⓒ Ⓓ

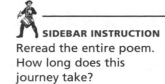

SIDEBAR INSTRUCTION
Reread the entire poem.
How long does this
journey take?

2 What is the theme of this poem?

A. rest

B. slumber

C. death

D. shelter

Ⓐ Ⓑ Ⓒ Ⓓ

SIDEBAR INSTRUCTION
Reread the entire poem
again. What is the main
idea?

3 The word *labor* in line 14 is best defined as meaning

A. manual labor.

B. people who provide care.

C. successful employment.

D. to dwell on something.

Ⓐ Ⓑ Ⓒ Ⓓ

SIDEBAR INSTRUCTION
Reread the last stanza
of the poem. The speaker
is referring to what type
of labor?

4 Which of the following figures of speech is used throughout this poem?

A. personification

B. oxymoron

C. symbolism

D. simile

Ⓐ Ⓑ Ⓒ Ⓓ

SIDEBAR INSTRUCTION
Sidebar Instruction: Think
about what this poem
really means. Does the
inn exist?

5 Lines 9 and 10 of the poem figuratively mean that

A. other wayfarers will be at the inn awaiting this traveler.

B. others have died before this traveler.

C. there will be a celebration at the inn.

D. there will be no one awaiting his arrival.

Ⓐ   Ⓑ   Ⓒ   Ⓓ

SIDEBAR INSTRUCTION
Carefully reread lines 9 and 10. Who will the traveler meet?

6 What is the mood of "Uphill"? Support your answer with details from the poem.

_____

_____

_____

_____

_____

_____

_____

_____

_____

STEP THREE ON YOUR OWN

Read the poem and answer the questions that follow.

I Wandered Lonely as a Cloud

William Wordsworth

1   I wandered lonely as a cloud
    That floats on high o'er vales and hills,
    When all at once I saw a crowd,
    A host, of golden daffodil;
    Beside the lake, beneath the trees,
6   Fluttering and dancing in the breeze.

    Continuous as the stars that shine
    And twinkle on the milky way,
    They stretched in never-ending line
    Along the margin of a bay:
    Ten thousand saw I at a glance,
12 Tossing their heads in sprightly dance.

    The waves beside them danced; but they
    Out-did the sparkling waves in glee:
    A poet could not but be gay,
    In such a jocund company:
    I gazed and gazed but little thought
18 What wealth the show to me had brought:

    For oft, when on my couch I lie
    In vacant or in pensive mood,
    They flash upon that inward eye
    Which is the bliss of solitude;
    And then my heart with pleasure fills,
24 And dances with the daffodils.

7 What is the rhyme scheme in the first stanza of "I Wandered Lonely as a Cloud"?

A. ABACCD

B. ABABCC

C. ABCDEE

D. ABABAB

Ⓐ Ⓑ Ⓒ Ⓓ

8 Which of the following figures of speech is used in lines 11 and 12?

A. metaphor

B. simile

C. personification

D. alliteration

Ⓐ Ⓑ Ⓒ Ⓓ

9 Lines 19–22 of "I Wandered Lonely as a Cloud" mean that

A. he often thinks about the daffodils.

B. he often visits the daffodils.

C. he frequently dances with the daffodils.

D. he wished he could keep the daffodils.

Ⓐ Ⓑ Ⓒ Ⓓ

10 The word *pensive* is best described as

A. sad.

B. meditative.

C. sentimental.

D. tired.

Ⓐ Ⓑ Ⓒ Ⓓ

11 What figure of speech is used in line 7 of the poem?

A. personification

B. simile

C. metaphor

D. analogy

Ⓐ Ⓑ Ⓒ Ⓓ

12 What is the theme of the poem "I Wandered Lonely as a Cloud"?
Support your answer with details from the poem.

_____

_____

_____

_____

_____

_____

_____

_____

_____

13 Explain how the title of this poem "I Wandered Lonely as a Cloud" is an example of both a simile and personification. Be specific in your explanation.

_____

_____

_____

_____

_____

_____

_____

_____

LESSON 9

Students will interpret the meaning of literary works, nonfiction, films, and media by using different critical lenses and analytic techniques.

WHAT THIS STANDARD MEANS

Questions for this standard will ask you to identify and analyze types of dramatic literature. You will be asked to analyze the elements and techniques used by a playwright. You will also be asked to analyze how dramatic conventions support, interpret, and enhance dramatic text.

STEP ONE **TEN-MINUTE LESSON**

Sample Passage

Excerpt from
A Doll's House

by Henrik Ibsen

1   **Maid**   *(in the doorway).* A lady's called, madam. A stranger.
Nora: Well, ask her to come in.
Maid: And the doctor's here too, sir.
Helmer: Has he gone to my room?
5   **Maid:**   Yes, sir.
  Helmer goes into his room. The Maid shows in Mrs. Linde,
  who is dressed in traveling clothes, and closes the door.
Mrs. Linde   *(shyly and a little hesitantly).* Good evening, Nora.
Nora   *(uncertainly).* Good evening—
10 **Mrs. Linde:**   I don't suppose you recognize me.
Nora: No, I'm afraid I—Yes, wait a minute—surely—*(Exclaims)*
  Why, Christine! Is it really you?
Mrs. Linde: Yes, it's me.
Nora: Christine! And I didn't recognize you! But how could I—?
15 *(More quietly.)* How you've changed, Christine!
Mrs. Linde: Yes, I know. It's been nine years—nearly ten—
Nora: Is it so long? Yes, it must be. Oh, these last eight years have been
  such a happy time for me! So you've come to town? All that way in
  winter! How brave of you!
20 **Mrs. Linde:**   I arrived by the steamer this morning.
Nora: Yes, of course—to enjoy yourself over Christmas. Oh, how
  splendid! We'll have to celebrate! But take off your coat. You're not
  cold, are you? *(Helps her off with it.)* There! Now let's sit down here
  by the stove and be comfortable. No, you take the armchair. I'll sit here
25 in the rocking-chair. *(Clasps Mrs. Linde's hands.)* Yes, now you look
  like your old self. It was just at first that—you've got a little paler,
  though, Christine. And perhaps a bit thinner.
Mrs. Linde: And older, Nora. Much, much older.
Nora: Yes, perhaps a little older. Just a tiny bit. Not much.

30   *(Checks herself suddenly and says earnestly.)* Oh, but how thoughtless of me to sit here and chatter away like this! Dear, sweet Christine, can you forgive me?

Mrs. Linde: What do you mean, Nora?

Nora *(quietly).* Poor Christine, you've become a widow.

35 **Mrs. Linde:**   Yes. Three years ago.

Nora: I know, I know—I read it in the papers. Oh, Christine, I meant to write to you so often, honestly. But I always put it off, and something else always cropped up.

Mrs. Linde: I understand, Nora dear.

40 **Nora:**   No, Christine, it was beastly of me. Oh, my poor darling, what you've gone through! And he didn't leave you anything?

Mrs. Linde: No.

Nora: No children, either?

Mrs. Linde: No.

45 **Nora:**   Nothing at all, then?

Mrs. Linde: Not even a feeling of loss or sorrow.

Nora *(looks incredulously at her).* But, Christine, how is that possible?

Mrs. Linde *(smiles sadly and strokes Nora's hair).* Oh, these things happen, Nora.

50 **Nora:**   All alone. How dreadful that must be for you. I've three lovely children. I'm afraid you can't see them now, because they're out with nanny. But you must tell me everything—

Mrs. Linde: No, no, no. I want to hear about you.

Nora: No, you start. I'm not going to be selfish today, I'm just going

55 to think about you. Oh, but there's one thing I *must* tell you. Have you heard of the wonderful luck we've just had?

Mrs. Linde: No. What?

Nora: Would you believe it—my husband's just been made manager of the bank!

60 **Mrs. Linde:**   Your husband? Oh, how lucky—!

Nora: Yes, isn't it? Being a lawyer is so uncertain, you know, especially if one isn't prepared to touch any case that isn't—well—quite nice. And of course Torvald's been very firm about that—and I'm absolutely with him. Oh, you can imagine how happy we are! He's joining the

65 bank in the New Year, and he'll be getting a big salary, and lots of percentages too. From now on we'll be able to live quite differently— we'll be able to do whatever we want. Oh, Christine, it's such a relief! I feel so happy! Well, I mean, it's lovely to have heaps of money and not to have to worry about anything. Don't you think?

70 **Mrs. Linde:**   It must be lovely to have enough to cover one's needs, anyway.

Nora: Not just our needs! We're going to have heaps and heaps of money!

Mrs. Linde   *(smiles).* Nora, Nora, haven't you grown up yet? When we

75 were at school you were a terrible little spendthrift.

Nora   *(laughs quietly).* Yes, Torvald still says that. *(Wags her finger.)* But "Nora, Nora" isn't as silly as you think. Oh, we've been in no position for me to waste money. We've both had to work.

Mrs. Linde: You too?

80 **Nora:**   Yes, little things—fancy work, crocheting, embroidery and so forth. *(Casually.)* And other things too. I suppose you know Torvald left the Ministry when we got married? There were no prospects of promotion in his department, and of course he needed more money. But the first year he overworked himself quite dreadfully. He had to

85 take on all sorts of extra jobs, and worked day and night. But it was too much for him, and he became frightfully ill. The doctors said he'd have to go to a warmer climate.

Mrs. Linde: Yes, you spent a whole year in Italy, didn't you?

Nora: Yes. It wasn't easy for me to get away, you know. I'd just had

90 Ivar. But of course we had to do it. Oh, it was a marvelous trip! And it saved Torvald's life. But it cost an awful lot of money, Christine.

Mrs. Linde: I can imagine.

Nora: Two hundred and fifty pounds. That's a lot of money, you know.

Mrs. Linde: How lucky you had it.

95 **Nora:**   Well, actually, we got it from my father.

Mrs. Linde: Oh, I see. Didn't he die just about that time?

Nora: Yes, Christine, just about then. Wasn't it dreadful, I couldn't go and look after him. I was expecting little Ivar any day. And then I had my poor Torvald to care for—we really didn't think he'd live. Dear,

100 kind Papa! I never saw him again, Christine. Oh, it's the saddest thing that's happened to me since I got married.

Sample Questions

1 How do Nora and Mrs. Linde react to each other in the excerpt?

A. wearily

B. kindly

C. defensively

D. strangely

Ⓐ   Ⓑ   Ⓒ   Ⓓ

This question asks you to consider how the two main characters react to each other. Reread the beginning of the excerpt. Are Nora and Mrs. Linde happy to see each other?

Answer choice A: Mrs. Linde may be weary, but Nora seems to have an abundance of energy. This is not the correct answer choice.

Answer choice B: Mrs. Linde is kind to Nora, and Nora at least tries to be kind to her. This is probably the correct answer choice but read all the answer choices to be sure.

Answer choice C: Neither woman seems to be defensive, so this is not the correct answer choice.

Answer choice D: Mrs. Linde does not behave strangely, and while Nora behaves self-centeredly, she does not really act strangely. Answer choice B is the best answer choice.

How does Nora's conversation with Mrs. Linde show readers that she is selfish? Use relevant details and information from the passage in your answer.

This is an open-response question. Nora knows that Mrs. Linde's husband died, yet she confesses that she did not even send her a card. Then she tells Mrs. Linde about her own husband and how happy she is with little regard to how this makes Mrs. Linde feel. She brags about her husband's promotion and does not even consider that Mrs. Linde has financial problems. She also tells Mrs. Linde that they spent a year in Italy on the money they inherited from her father. While her father was dying, she did not even go and look after him.

STEP TWO **SIDEBAR INSTRUCTION**

Read the passage and answer the questions that follow. Use the Sidebar Instruction to help you choose the best answer.

Excerpt from
The Sound of a Voice
by David Henry Hwang

1   **MAN:**   How long has it been since you last had
    a visitor? *(Pause).*
  WOMAN: I don't know.
  MAN: Oh?
5   **WOMAN:**   I lose track. Perhaps five months
    ago, perhaps ten years, perhaps yesterday.
    I don't consider time when there is no voice
    in the air. It's pointless. Time begins with the
    entrance of a visitor, and ends with his exit.
10   **MAN:**   And in between? You don't keep track
    of the days? You can't help but notice—
  WOMAN: Of course I notice.
  MAN: Oh.
  WOMAN: I notice, but I don't keep track.
15   *(Pause).* May I bring out more?
  MAN: More? No. No. This was wonderful.
  WOMAN: I have more.
  MAN: Really—the best I've had.
  WOMAN: You must be tired. Did you sleep in
20   the forest last night?
  MAN: Yes.
  WOMAN: Or did you not sleep at all?
  MAN: I slept.
  WOMAN: Where?
25   **MAN:**   By a waterfall. The sound of the water put me to sleep.
    It rumbled like the sounds of a city. You see, I can't sleep in too much
    silence. It scares me. It makes me feel that I have no control over
    what is about to happen.
  WOMAN: I feel the same way.

1 What can you tell about the woman from lines 5–9?

A. She is afraid of the future.

B. She has been alone a long time.

C. She is relieved to speak to someone.

D. She has moved from place to place.

Ⓐ Ⓑ Ⓒ Ⓓ

SIDEBAR INSTRUCTION
Reread these lines. Why does the woman say she has trouble keeping track of time?

2 Pauses are used in this selection to

A. stress the importance of the dialogue.

B. separate thoughts from dialogue.

C. indicate stage directions.

D. enhance the atmosphere between the MAN and the WOMAN.

Ⓐ Ⓑ Ⓒ Ⓓ

SIDEBAR INSTRUCTION
Look at where the pauses are inserted. What effect do they have?

3 The woman in the excerpt can best be described as

A. lonely.

B. angry.

C. suspicious.

D. annoyed.

Ⓐ Ⓑ Ⓒ Ⓓ

SIDEBAR INSTRUCTION
Reread the excerpt. How does the woman respond to the man?

4 The woman believes that time begins

A. when noise is heard.

B. when someone visits.

C. when something happens.

D. when she is by a waterfall.

Ⓐ   Ⓑ   Ⓒ   Ⓓ

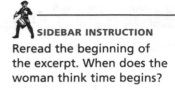
SIDEBAR INSTRUCTION
Reread the beginning of the excerpt. When does the woman think time begins?

5 The man likes to sleep with noise because

A. it calms his spirit.

B. it clears his mind.

C. it makes him feel in control.

D. it blocks out other sounds.

Ⓐ   Ⓑ   Ⓒ   Ⓓ

SIDEBAR INSTRUCTION
Reread the end of the excerpt. Why does the man like to sleep with noise?

6 Speculate on whether or not you think the man and woman are old friends or if they have just met each other. Give support to your answer.

STEP THREE ON YOUR OWN

Read the passage and answer the questions that follow.

From
PYGMALION*
by Bernard Shaw

1   **THE SARCASTIC BYSTANDER**   I can tell where you come from. You come from Anwell. Go back there.
  THE NOTE TAKER   (*helpfully*) Hanwell.
  THE SARCASTIC BYSTANDER   (*affecting great distinction of speech*)
5   Thenk you, teacher. Haw haw! So long (*he touches his hat with mock respect and strolls off*).
  THE FLOWER GIRL   Frightening people like that! How would he like it himself.
  THE MOTHER   It's quite fine now, Clara. We can walk to a motor bus.
10   Come. (*She gathers her skirts above her ankles and hurries off towards the Strand*).
  THE DAUGHTER   But the cab—(*her mother is out of hearing*). Oh, how tiresome! (*She follows angrily*).
  All the rest have gone except the note taker, the gentleman, and the flower
15   *girl, who sits arranging her basket, and still pitying herself in murmurs.*
  THE FLOWER GIRL   Poor girl! Hard enough for her to live without being worrited and chivied.
  THE GENTLEMAN   (*returning to his former place on the note taker's left*) How do you do it, if I may ask?
20   **THE NOTE TAKER**   Simply phonetics. The science of speech. That's my profession: also my hobby. Happy is the man who can make a living by his hobby! You can spot an Irishman or a Yorkshireman by his brogue. I can place any man within six miles. I can place him within two miles in London. Sometimes within two streets.
25   **THE FLOWER GIRL**   Ought to be ashamed of himself, unmanly coward!
  THE GENTLEMAN   But is there a living in that?

160

THE NOTE TAKER   Oh yes. Quite a fat one. This is an age of upstarts.
Men begin in Kentish Town with £80 a year, and end in Park Lane
30   with a hundred thousand. They want to drop Kentish Town; but they
give themselves away every time they open their mouths. Now I can
teach them—

THE FLOWER GIRL   Let him mind his own business and leave a poor
girl—

35   **THE NOTE TAKER**   (*explosively*) Woman: cease this detestable
boohooing instantly; or else seek the shelter of some other place of
worship.

THE FLOWER GIRL   (*with feeble defiance*) I've a right to be here if I
like, same as you.

40   **THE NOTE TAKER**   A woman who
utters   such   depressing   and
disgusting sounds has no right to be
anywhere—no   right   to   live.
Remember that you are a human
45   being with a soul and the divine gift
of articulate speech: that your native
language   is   the   language   of
Shakespear and Milton and The
Bible; and don't sit there crooning
50   like a bilious pigeon.

THE   FLOWER   GIRL   (*quite
overwhelmed, and looking up at him
in mingled wonder and deprecation
without daring to raise her head*)
55   Ah-ah-ah-ow-ow-ow-oo!

THE NOTE TAKER   (*whipping out
his book*) Heavens! what a sound!
(*He writes; then holds out the book
and reads, reproducing her vowels
60   exactly*) Ah-ah-ah-ow-ow-ow-oo!

THE FLOWER GIRL   (*tickled by
the performance, and laughing in
spite of herself*) Garn!

THE NOTE TAKER   You see this creature with her kerbstone English:
65   the English that will keep her in the gutter to the end of her days. Well,
sir, in three months I could pass that girl off as a duchess at an
ambassador's garden party. I could even get her a place as lady's maid or
shop assistant, which requires better English…

---

* NOTE: this excerpt is about people discussing language. Some of the words have
been purposely spelled in unusual ways to show how the characters speak.

7 What can you tell about the flower girl in this story?

A. She has met the note taker before.

B. She was not born in England.

C. She feels sorry for herself.

D. She has studied many languages.

Ⓐ Ⓑ Ⓒ Ⓓ

Read the lines in the box below.

> **THE NOTE TAKER** …They want to drop Kentish Town; but they give themselves away every time they open their mouths. Now I can teach them—
>
> **THE FLOWER GIRL** Let him mind his own business and leave a poor girl—

8 What is the purpose of the dashes in the above statements?

A. to show that the flower girl is interrupting the note taker

B. to emphasize the many things the note taker is talking about

C. to draw attention to the unusual way the flower girl speaks

D. to suggest that the flower girl is speaking to herself

Ⓐ Ⓑ Ⓒ Ⓓ

9 According to the excerpt, what is the note taker's primary reason for being a speech scientist?

A. He likes to help people move up in society.

B. He enjoys making a lot of money.

C. He loves studying phonetics.

D. He delights in correcting people.

Ⓐ Ⓑ Ⓒ Ⓓ

10 Which word **best** describes the gentleman in the excerpt of the play?

A. arrogant

B. inquisitive

C. doubtful

D. deceitful

Ⓐ Ⓑ Ⓒ Ⓓ

Read the stage directions in the box below.

> *(affecting great distinction of speech)*

11 What does this stage direction tell the reader about the sarcastic bystander?

A. He is not sure of what he is saying.

B. He is speaking too quietly to be heard by the others.

C. He is very excited about meeting the note taker.

D. He is pretending to speak in an elegant way.

Ⓐ Ⓑ Ⓒ Ⓓ

This section reviews the standards you have just learned. The questions in this review are for Standards 12, 14, and 17. Read the passages and answer the questions that follow.

Passage 1

Filling Station

by Elizabeth Bishop

1 On, but it is dirty!
    —this little filling station,
    oil-soaked, oil-permeated
    to a disturbing, over-all
    black translucency.
6 Be careful with that match!

    Father wears a dirty,
    oil-soaked monkey suit
    that cuts him under the arms,
    and several quick and saucy
    and greasy sons assist him
    (it's a family filling station),
13 all quite thoroughly dirty.

    Do they live in the station?
    It has a cement porch
    behind the pumps, and on it
    a set of crushed and grease-
    impregnated wickerwork;
    on the wicker sofa
20 a dirty dog, quite comfy.

Some comic books provide
the only note of color—
of certain color. They lie
upon a big dim doily
draping a taboret*
(part of the set), beside
27   a big hirsute begonia.

Why the extraneous plant?
Why the taboret?
Why, oh why, the doily?
(Embroidered in daisy stitch
with marguerites,* I think,
33   and heavy with gray crochet.)

Somebody embroidered the doily.
Somebody waters the plant,
or oils it, maybe. Somebody
37   arranges the rows of cans

so that they softly say:
ESSO*—so—so—so
to high-strung automobiles.
41   Somebody loves us all.

---

*taboret: small table
*marguerites: daisies
*ESSO: a type of gasoline

1 What is the main idea expressed throughout the poem about the filling station?

A. It is very dirty.

B. It has a porch.

C. It has a doily.

D. It has comic books.

Ⓐ Ⓑ Ⓒ Ⓓ

2 Which of the following figures of speech is used in line 39?

A. personification

B. analogy

C. metaphor

D. alliteration

Ⓐ Ⓑ Ⓒ Ⓓ

3 What does the author consider to be out of place at the filling station?

A. the dog

B. the sons

C. the comic books

D. the doily

Ⓐ Ⓑ Ⓒ Ⓓ

4 Which figure of speech is used the **most** throughout the poem?

A. hyperbole

B. imagery

C. simile

D. metaphor

Ⓐ Ⓑ Ⓒ Ⓓ

Passage 2

from
The Gap

by Eugene Ionesco

(translated by Rosette Lamont)

1   **The Wife.**   Dear friend, tell me all.
     The Friend.   I don't know what to say.
     The Wife.   I know.
     The Friend.   I hear the news last night. I did not want to call you. At the
5   same time I couldn't wait any longer. Please forgive me for coming so
     early with such terrible news.
     The Wife.   He didn't make it! How terrible! We were still hoping. . . .
     The Friend.   It's hard, I know. He still had a chance. Not much of one.
     We had to expect it.
10   **The Wife.**   I didn't expect it. He was always so successful. He could
     always manage somehow, at the last moment.
     The Friend.   In that state of exhaustion. You shouldn't have let him!
     The Wife.   What can we do, what can we do! . . . How awful!
     The Friend.   Come on, dear friend, be brave. That's life.
15   **The Wife.**   I feel faint: I'm going to faint. (She falls in one of the armchairs.)
     The Friend.   (Holding her, gently slapping her cheeks and hands.)
     I shouldn't have blurted it out like that. I'm sorry.
     The Wife.   No, you were right to do so. I had to find out somehow or other.
     The Friend.   I should have prepared you carefully.
20   **The Wife.**   I've got to be strong. I can't help thinking of him, the wretched
     man. I hope they won't put it in the papers. Can we count on the
     journalists' discretion?
     The Friend.   Close your door. Don't answer the telephone. It will still get
     around. You could go to the country. In a couple of months, when you
25   are better, you'll come back, you'll go on with your life. People forget
     such things.

166

The Wife.   People won't forget so fast. That's all they were waiting for. Some friends will feel sorry, but the others. . . . (The Academician*
comes in, fully dressed: uniform, chest covered with decorations, his
30   sword on his side.)

The Academician.   Up so early, my dear? (To **The Friend.**) You've come early too. What's happening? Do you have the final results?

The Wife.   What a disgrace!

The Friend.   You mustn't crush him like this, dear friend. (To **The**
35   **Academician.**) You have failed.

The Academician.   Are you quite sure?

The Friend.   You should never have tried to pass the baccalaureate examination.

The Academician.   They failed me. The rats! How dare they do this to me!

40   **The Friend.**   The marks were posted late in the evening.

The Academician.   Perhaps it was difficult to make them out in the dark. How could you read them?

The Friend.   They had set up spotlights.

The Academician.   They're doing everything to ruin me.

45   **The Friend.**   I passed by in the morning; the marks were still up.

The Academician.   You could have bribed the concierge into pulling them down.

The Friend.   That's exactly what I did. Unfortunately the police were there. Your name heads the list of those who failed. Everyone's standing
50   in line to get a look. There's an awful crush.

The Academician.   Who's there? The parents of the candidates?

The Friend.   Not only they.

The Wife.   All your rivals, all your colleagues must be there. All those you attacked in the press for ignorance: your undergraduates, your
55   graduate students, all those you failed when you were chairman of the board of examiners.

The Academician.   I am discredited! But I won't let them. There must be some mistake.

The Friend.   I saw the examiners. I spoke with them. They gave me your
60   marks. Zero in the mathematics.

The Academician.   I had no scientific training.

The Friend.   Zero in Greek, zero in Latin.

The Wife.   (to her husband). You, a humanist, the spokesman for humanism, the author of that famous treatise "The Defense of Poesy
65   and Humanism."

The Academician.   I beg your pardon, but my book concerns itself with twentieth century humanism. (To **The Friend.**) What about composition? What grade did I get in composition?

The Friend.   Nine hundred. You have nine hundred points.

70   **The Academician.**   That's perfect. My average must be all the way up.

The Friend.   Unfortunately not. They're marking on the basis of two thousand. The passing grade is one thousand.

The Academician.   They must have changed the regulations.

167

The Wife. They didn't change them just for you. You have a frightful
75 persecution complex.
The Academician. I tell you they changed them.
The Friend. They went back to the old ones, back to the time of
Napoleon.
The Academician. Utterly outmoded. Besides, when did they make those
80 changes? It isn't legal. I'm chairman of the Baccalaureate Commission of
the Ministry of Public Education. They didn't consult me, and they
cannot make any changes without my approval. I'm going to expose
them. I'm going to bring government charges against them.
The Wife. Darling, you don't know what you're doing. You're in your
85 dotage*. Don't you recall handing in your resignation just before taking
the examination so that no one could doubt the complete objectivity of
the board of examiners?
The Academician. I'll take it back.
The Wife. You should never have taken that test. I warned you. After all,
90 it's not as if you needed it. But you have to collect all the honors, don't
you? You're never satisfied. What did you need this diploma for? Now all
is lost. You have your Doctorate, your Master's, your high school
diploma, your elementary school certificate, and even the first part of
the baccalaureate.

---

*academician - a scholar or professor
*dotage – memory problems due to old age

5 What is the main conflict in the scene?

A. The wife is struggling to help the academician remember his past.

B. The academician refuses to believe he failed the test.

C. The friend is working to ruin the academician's reputation.

D. The academician's rivals are trying to find ways to lower his score.

Ⓐ Ⓑ Ⓒ Ⓓ

6 Which of the following is the wife's concern?

A. She wants the Baccalaureate Commission to use modern standards.

B. She wants the friend to hide the bad news from the academician.

C. She does not want their social standing to be harmed.

D. She does not want to believe that her husband is not a great scholar.

Ⓐ Ⓑ Ⓒ Ⓓ

7 How does the wife's character contrast with the academician's character?

A. She wants to blame him while he wants to blame his rivals.

B. She wants to learn the truth while he wants to hide it.

C. She is humble while he is arrogant.

D. She is honest while he is deceitful.

Ⓐ Ⓑ Ⓒ Ⓓ

8 What does the wife mean when she says that the academician has "a frightful persecution complex"?

A. The academician has a fear of being wrong.

B. The academician believes everyone is working against him.

C. The academician is afraid of being unsuccessful.

D. The wife and the academician are cruel to one another.

Ⓐ Ⓑ Ⓒ Ⓓ

9 Identify two of the academician's flaws as a result of his reaction to the bad news. What does this say about his character? Use relevant and specific information from the excerpt to support your answer.

_____

_____

_____

_____

_____

_____

_____

_____

_____

LESSON 10

Students will identify, analyze, and apply knowledge of the structure, elements, and meaning of nonfiction or informational material and provide evidence from the text to support their understanding.

WHAT THIS STANDARD MEANS

Questions assessing this standard will ask you to analyze the structure and elements of nonfiction passages. You may be asked how and why the author presents information in the passage. You may also be asked to determine an author's meaning in part of or all of a passage.

STEP ONE **TEN-MINUTE LESSON**

Sample Passage

from Flying Sharks:
powerful hunters of False Bay
by David George Gordon

1   Racing upward from the depths, a great white shark suddenly bursts from the water, launching itself into the air. The "flying" shark's target? A Cape fur seal swimming at the surface of False Bay off the coast of South Africa.

2   An attacking great white shark can cut through the water at 35 miles an hour—seven times faster than the best Olympic swimmer.

3   "At that speed, the shark may flip tail over head in midair, completing a somersault before hitting the water," says R. Aidan Martin, one of several shark experts now studying this unusual behavior. "That's an awesome sight!"

4   Great white sharks are among the most fearsome predators in the sea. They come to Seal Island in South Africa's False Bay to snack on the seals that live there by the thousands. Silently the sharks patrol, waiting for an opportunity to attack and fill their bellies with red, fat-rich seal meat.

5   Onshore, the seals bask on the rocks of their island sanctuary. Eventually they must leave land to hunt for squid, fish, and other food from the sea. They seem to know the danger that lurks offshore. Seeking safety in numbers, the seals gather in groups of about a dozen. Then, quick as a flash, they dive into the water, swimming as fast as they can toward the mouth of the bay. Sometimes for the seals, however, it's not fast enough.

6   The first half-mile from shore proves deadliest. Martin and other shark watchers call this stretch the "Ring of Death." "That's where most of the shark attacks—as many as 25 in one day—take place," Martin explains.

7   The seals have keen eyesight. "If they are lucky, they might look down into the water and see a shark heading their way," says Martin. "But often they haven't a clue until it's too late."

Sample Questions

1 What does the author do to illustrate the swimming speed of the great white shark?

A. He says they dive as "quick as a Bash."

B. He compares their movement to a lightning bolt.

C. He compares their speed to that of an Olympic swimmer.

D. He explains that most shark attacks occur near the shore.

Ⓐ   Ⓑ   Ⓒ   Ⓓ

This question asks you to examine the author's methods of conveying ideas. The author wants to introduce the reader to great white sharks and the way they hunt the seals of False Bay. The most important information he wants to convey, though, is how fast great white sharks can swim. How does he do that in the selection? If you don't remember, refer back to the selection and look for the information.

Answer choice A: Does the author say that sharks dive as "quick as a Bash"? He does use that phrase in the selection, but if you look carefully, you will see that he's describing the seals and not the sharks. The seals have to move fast to avoid the sharks. There is probably a better answer choice.

Answer choice B: A lightning bolt is definitely fast, but the author does not use any comparison between a lightning bolt and sharks. You can eliminate this answer choice.

Answer choice C: Is a shark's speed comparable to the speed of an Olympic swimmer? The author tells us that sharks swim seven times faster than the best Olympians—and that's fast! This is a great illustration of the speed of a great white shark. This is probably the best answer choice, but you should read the next choice just to make sure.

Answer choice D: The author does say that most shark attacks occur near the shore. He also says that sharks swim very fast. But are these two ideas connected? No, they are separate ideas about shark behavior. Now you can be certain that the best answer choice is C.

2 What is the author trying to establish in paragraph 7?

A. He wants to emphasize that the waters of South Africa are very clear.

B. He begins to discuss the seals of False Bay.

C. He describes the "Ring of Death."

D. He intends is to show that the seals have some defense against the sharks.

Ⓐ Ⓑ Ⓒ Ⓓ

To answer this question, you need to look at a part of the selection and decide what is its main purpose. In paragraph 7, the author says that seals have "keen eyesight." He also shares some of shark expert R. Aidan Martin's comments on the seals' eyesight. Read this paragraph and then read the answer choices. What is the author trying to convey in paragraph 7?

Answer choice A: Is the author commenting on the clarity of South African water? The seals may be able to see the sharks because the water is clear and clean. However, this is probably not the point the author hoped to make. There is probably a better answer choice.

Answer choice B: Does the author's statement about the seals' eyesight suggest that he's going to describe the seals of False Bay? Think about the title and main ideas. This selection is about sharks. The author seems to describe the seals only enough to help the reader learn about the sharks. The seals are not the main point of this selection, so this is probably not the best answer choice.

Answer choice C: The author mentions that many seals are hunted in a so-called "Ring of Death." Is the author going to describe that in more detail? Think about what you've just read. The author is focusing on the sharks, and he's already described the "Ring of Death." He doesn't have a good reason to return to the topic, so this is not the best answer choice.

Answer choice D: Is the author saying that the seals are not totally defenseless against the sharks? Although the seals are slower than the sharks and can't always see them, the seals' eyesight gives them some defense. The author seems to be making the point that the seals are not completely helpless. After reading the other choices, you now know that D is the best answer choice.

STEP TWO — SIDEBAR INSTRUCTION

Read the selection and answer the questions that follow. Use the Sidebar Instruction to help you choose the correct answer.

'Inverted Jenny'
stamps on display at National Postal Museum in D.C.

by Scott McCaffrey

1   **WASHINGTON**– To stamp collectors, it's known by the catalog designation "C3a." To non-collectors, it's known as "the stamp with the upside-down airplane."

2   It's the most famous American postage stamp ever, a 1918 24-cent airmail adhesive which was printed incorrectly. A single sheet of 100 "Inverted Jenny" stamps made its way into collectors' hands, and today a single example from that pane can trade hands for more than $100,000.

3   Nearly a quarter of those stamps will be on display July 30 through September 30 at the National Postal Museum in Washington, D.C., as the Smithsonian Institution celebrates the error with a special exhibit.

4   Called the "Jenny Class Reunion," the exhibition brings together the Smithsonian's single invert with 22 more on loan from private sources. It is the biggest exhibit in the postal museum's three-year history.

5   "We had help from a lot of philatelists* and stamp dealers; it did require some sleuthing," Daisy Ridgway, the museum's spokeswoman, said of putting the exhibit together.

6   This isn't the largest collection of the inverts ever under one roof—more than 35 were exhibited at a large stamp show in the 1980s—but it is the most ever collected for a single exhibit.

7   "It's very well protected," Ridgway said of the Jenny exhibition. "We have a large security force on hand at all times."

8   The Post Office Department—forerunner of today's Postal Service—issued the 24 cent stamp on May 13, 1918. It was produced to pay postage and special delivery charges for the

government's fledgling air mail service between New York, Philadelphia and Boston.

9   A day later, stamp collector William T. Robey sniffed out the possibility of an error. Robey went to a Washington post office and purchased a sheet of 100 airmail stamps, no small purchase those days. The stamps were printed correctly.

10   According to the legend that has grown up around the stamp, Robey soon returned to purchase another sheet. The clerk handed one over, and Robey discovered to his delight that the blue color—depicting a Curtiss JN-4 "Jenny" airplane—and the carmine (red) frame had been printed in different directions.

11   How did it happen? The stamp was engraved, with the paper run through two separate presses, one for each of the two colors. Midway through the process, apparently during an inspection, Robey's sheet was inadvertently turned around.

12   Since the blue plane was printed first, it's most accurate to say the frame is upside-down from the plane, although collectors and non-collectors alike refer to the stamp as having an upside-down plane.

13   The stamp was printed during World War I, when the Bureau of Engraving and Printing was overwhelmed with postage and revenue stamp production. The 24-cent Jenny was rushed into print, taking only 9 days from production of the printing plates to completion of the press run. With that type of schedule, it might be more amazing that only one sheet of error stamps escaped to the general public.

14   When word of the error leaked out, government officials tried various threats to get Robey's stamps back, but the collector refused to budge—with good reason. He quickly sold the sheet to a big-name stamp collector for $15,000, and it quickly was re-sold for $20,000 to eccentric millionaire and stamp accumulator Edward Green.

15   The latter collector separated the sheet into single stamps and blocks of four. Today, a well-centered example with its original gum can sell for more than $100,000.

16   Collectors have tracked the whereabouts of all the stamps for years. Only a couple have disappeared from public view, including two that were stolen and have not resurfaced. The Smithsonian

acquired its stamp about three decades ago, but it is not continuously displayed, since lighting causes the red frame to dull.

17   New technology will help the situation. The postal museum has installed special fiber-optic lighting for the exhibit, which cuts down on direct glare.

18   "The carmine of this stamp is prone to fading, and the fiber-optic lighting reflects off the dark canvas, then back onto the stamp," Ridgway said. "It will enable us to keep stamps like this on display a longer time."

19   For those who think inverted stamps are a thing of the past, two major U.S. errors—one involving the Richard Nixon commemorative stamp—have surfaced in the past decade. Neither has yet achieved the fame, or the price tag, of the Inverted Jenny.

20   The Post Office Department once even printed 40 million stamps in error—on purpose.

21   When some copies of the 1962 commemorative honoring Dag Hammarskjold were found by collectors with the yellow printing upside-down, post office officials ordered the error repeated on millions of stamps to deflate the value of the errors. Today, a Hammarskjold "error" can be purchased for just pennies, not thousands.

22   The National Postal Museum has several other displays of air mail material, including several mail planes. Oddly, the inaugural air mail flight experienced similar bad luck to the stamp printed for it.

23   On May 15, 1918, while piloting a Jenny air mail flight from Washington to New York, Army Lt. George L. Boyle became disoriented and was forced down in a Maryland field. The plane's mail load was transported to New York a day later.

24   The exhibit is part of the Smithsonian's 150th anniversary celebrations, which are going on all year. The postal museum is home to 16 million items; only a small percentage are on display at any one time.

---

* philatelists – collectors of stamps

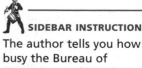

1 According to the author, the Jenny stamp was "rushed into print" in only nine days. What does he say might be remarkable about that fact?

A. The stamps were printed quickly, but they're still famous eighty years later.

B. A Jenny plane carrying the first delivery of air mail with the new stamps became lost during its mail route.

C. Despite the hurried schedule, only one sheet of error stamps reached the public.

D. The speed of the printing caused the carmine ink to fade.

Ⓐ   Ⓑ   Ⓒ   Ⓓ

SIDEBAR INSTRUCTION
The author tells you how busy the Bureau of Engraving and Printing was when it made these stamps. What does he say happened that was hard to believe?

2 In paragraph 1, the author gives two names for the Jenny stamp. His main reason for doing this is probably to

A. describe an important stamp in everyday terms.

B. compare stamp collectors to people with little knowledge of stamps.

C. show that this stamp is treasured by collectors.

D. introduce two names that will be used frequently in the selection.

Ⓐ   Ⓑ   Ⓒ   Ⓓ

 SIDEBAR INSTRUCTION
Reread the opening of the selection. The author writes that the stamp has a catalog code but has a common name because it features an upside-down airplane. Think about what that statement conveys to you. What is the author's intent?

3 The author writes that, in 1918, William T. Robey bought 100 airmail stamps, which was "no small purchase those days." What is the author implying with that phrase?

A. The sheet of stamps was very large and difficult to transport.

B. Robey expected the stamps' value to increase over the coming years.

C. Robey seemed strange then because he bought so many stamps.

D. Air mail stamps were expensive in 1918.

Ⓐ   Ⓑ   Ⓒ   Ⓓ

 SIDEBAR INSTRUCTION
Think about the phrase "no small purchase those days." What is he saying about the purchase of air mail stamps in 1918? Compare this to modern times.

Read the sentence from paragraph 14 in the box below.

> [Robey] quickly sold the sheet to a
> big-name stamp collector for $15,000,
> and it quickly was re-sold for $20,000
> to eccentric millionaire and stamp
> accumulator Edward Green.

4 Which of the following **best** summarizes the purpose of this statement?

A. Robey quickly became famous for his purchase.

B. The stamps skyrocketed in value.

C. The stamps have had many previous owners.

D. Money has less value today than in 1918.

Ⓐ Ⓑ Ⓒ Ⓓ

SIDEBAR INSTRUCTION
Read over this sentence from the selection carefully. It lists the second and third times the stamps were sold. What is the most important detail in this sentence?

5 In paragraphs 20–21, the author explains that the Post Office Department once continued to print an error stamp on purpose. According to the author, what does this suggest about the Post Office Department?

A. It tries to discourage collectors from paying huge amounts for error stamps.

B. It hopes to create interest by purposely producing error stamps.

C. It cannot stop its stamp printing machines even after it discovers an error.

D. It accidentally creates many error stamps every year.

Ⓐ Ⓑ Ⓒ Ⓓ

SIDEBAR INSTRUCTION
Go back to the selection and read over paragraphs 20–21. They talk about the famous Dag Hammarskjold stamp, which was printed even though an error was discovered. Why does the author say this was done?

STEP THREE **ON YOUR OWN**

Read the following passage and answer the questions that follow.

from The **mountain goat** foments trouble in a fragile paradise

by Charles Bergman

1   A big billy, white-bearded and suspicious, ambled onto the ridge below Mt. Angeles. He paused at the edge of the 40-by-40-foot net suspended on poles like a tent for a religious revival. Barely 20 feet away, he looked at us, sniffed the misty air and licked the nylon net with a thick black tongue.

2   "Now?"

3   "No. Wait till he gets to the center."

4   But he drifted out from under the net and into the subalpine fir forest. In a moment he made another pass under the edges of the net. Attracted to the buckets of salt in the center, he barely reached them on the third pass when a voice called out "Now!"

5   Two men jerked the pull ropes. The net collapsed. Before it hit the goat, he had already made three leaps toward the outer edges. In the same few seconds, the crew of biologists and park rangers sprang onto the bounding goat. He was one of the biggest they had ever caught, about 250 pounds, and it took four men to wrestle him to the ground. One man slipped pieces of green garden hose over the goat's stiletto-sharp horns, another hobbled his hooves, and two more covered his bronze eyes with a blue-denim mask.

6   We caught the goat because he did not belong here. Mt. Angeles is in the Olympic Mountains, one of the many peaks in the

1,400-square-mile wilderness of Washington's Olympic National Park. The problem is that mountain goats are not native to this area. Nearly 100,000 goats inhabit craggy cliffs and alpine meadows throughout the Northwest, from Washington, Idaho and Montana northward into Alaska. But for interesting geological reasons, the Olympic Mountains, in the extreme northwestern corner of the contiguous United States, were one of the ranges without goats until a dozen were introduced about 60 years ago. Those few goats found the Olympics congenial, ideally suited to their needs, and their population exploded. Now, there are more than 1,000 goats in the park.

7   Inspired by the peaks scarfed with snow, an early explorer named the highest peak Mt. Olympus after the ancient Greek "Home of the Gods." But putting mountain goats here turned out to be like putting Rototillers in heaven. They are chewing up the plant life and digging up the meadows. Although the mountain goats seem to epitomize Olympic National Park, they are nevertheless "exotics" and they have upset the delicate ecological balance of the wilderness system.

8   In an attempt to solve the goat problem, park biologists have developed a four-year experimental management project that includes capturing wild goats under drop nets and transferring them, in boxes dangling by cables from a helicopter, out of the park. Even more remarkable and innovative, they are experimenting with two kinds of birth control: hormone implants for some nannies to inhibit estrus* and in-the-field surgical sterilization for others.

9   Bruce Moorhead, wildlife management biologist for Olympic National Park, was the early prophet of the problems caused by the goats. He calls the proliferation* of exotic species "one of the most significant wildlife dilemmas in the world." The problem is especially intense for our National Park Service.

---

* inhibit estrus – causes an animal to not want to mate

* proliferation – rapid spread of a population

6 The **main** purpose of this selection is to

A. argue that the removal of the billy goats is unnecessary.

B. analyze the habits and environment of the mountain goats.

C. explain the problem of 'exotic' goats in a national park.

D. tell the story of how four men captured a billy goat.

Ⓐ   Ⓑ   Ⓒ   Ⓓ

7 In paragraph 6, the author says that the goat "population exploded." What does he mean by that phrase?

A. The goat population quickly increased.

B. The goat population was drastically reduced.

C. The goats were herded and moved to another area.

D. The goats mingled with other animals.

Ⓐ   Ⓑ   Ⓒ   Ⓓ

8 The author likely included the dialogue in paragraphs 2 and 3 in order to convey a sense of

A. fear.

B. suspence.

C. confusion.

D. sorrow.

Ⓐ   Ⓑ   Ⓒ   Ⓓ

9 What evidence does the author use to show how hard biologists are working to control the goat problem?

A. The author states that the goats are chewing and digging up the plants on the meadows.

B. The author explains that in sixty years the goat population has gone from 12 to 1,000.

C. The author describes how exotic species are an intense problem for the National Park Service.

D. The author tells how relocation and birth control are used to reduce the goat population.

Ⓐ   Ⓑ   Ⓒ   Ⓓ

LESSON 11

Students will identify and analyze how an author's choice of words appeals to the senses, creates imagery, suggests mood, and sets tone.

WHAT THIS STANDARD MEANS

Questions assessed by this benchmark will ask you to analyze how authors use words to appeal to the senses. Questions will determine why he or she used certain words and phrases that create imagery, suggest mood, or set the tone.

STEP ONE **TEN-MINUTE LESSON**

Sample Passage

SOUNDER

by William Armstrong

1   With the flavor of hand and biscuit still in his mouth, the boy felt good. He watched his mother as she patched his father's overalls with a piece of ticking. The combination of faded blue overall cloth and gray-and-white-striped ticking looked odd. One time at the meetin'-house picnic, boys with patches the same color as their overalls had laughed at him and pointed to the checkered gingham on the knees of his overalls. He had felt mad and hurt. But his mother had said, "Pay no mind, child," and had led him away. He hoped no one would laugh at his father. His father wouldn't be hurt. He didn't get hurt. He would get mad and fight back, and the boy was always afraid when his father got mad.

2   When the woman had patched the torn place, she got the walnut basket, folded her apron in her lap, and began to pick out the golden-brown kernels. The boy thought she would sing, but the rocker only moved enough to squeak. She hummed softly, and her lips looked glued together. "Look down, look down that lonesome road." The boy wished she would stop humming and tell a story about the Lord or King David, but she kept humming "That Lonesome Road."

3   The boy decided it was lonesomer in bed in the dark than it was staying up. He was glad he could sit a long time after the young children had gone to bed. Once he had been gathering weeds which his father had cut at the edge of a lawn. On the lawn a lady sat under a tree reading a story aloud to some children. He wished his mother or father could read. And if they had a book, he would hold the lamp by the chair so they could see the words and never get tired. "One day I will learn to read," he said to himself. He would have a book with stories in it, then he wouldn't be lonesome even if his mother didn't sing.

Sample Questions

1 What is the main effect of the author saying the mother's "lips looked glued together" in paragraph 2?

A. The main effect shows that she wasn't eating the walnuts.

B. The main effect creates an image of her concentrating on her task.

C. The main effect emphasizes that she is preoccupied.

D. The main effect is that it makes her seem mysterious.

Ⓐ   Ⓑ   Ⓒ   Ⓓ

This question asks you to examine the author's choice of words. The author might have described the mother in many different ways using many different words, but he chose to say that her lips seemed "glued together." Using what you know about the mother and her son, think about why the author might have emphasized that detail. Read the answer choices and see which explanation fits best.

Answer choice A: The story tells us that the mother was sorting through a basket of walnuts. Does the author want to remind us that she's not eating the walnuts? This seems unlikely because that information wouldn't apply to the story. You can eliminate this answer choice.

Answer choice B: Does the image of the mother's lips glued together show that she is concentrating on the walnuts? Sorting walnuts probably does not require much concentration, and the boy expects her to sing or talk while sorting walnuts. This is probably not the best answer choice.

Answer choice C: The boy is hoping that his mother will tell stories or sing songs while sitting on the rocking chair. Instead, she sits quietly humming. This disappoints the boy. The author is most likely using the image of her lips glued together to emphasize that she is preoccupied. This is probably the best choice, but look at the last choice to make sure.

Answer choice D: Does the mother seem like a mysterious character with closed lips? She is active and resourceful, and she tells stories and sings. She does not seem very mysterious. The best answer choice is C.

2 What image is created by the author using *ticking* and *patches* in paragraph 1?

A. uniformity

B. poverty

C. strength

D. hopelessness

Ⓐ   Ⓑ   Ⓒ   Ⓓ

This question asks you to analyze how the author uses imagery in this excerpt. Think about what was said about the ticking and patches that the mother used to fix the family's clothing. The boy remembered it as being of a mismatched color that looked odd and caused him to be ridiculed. What idea is the author trying to convey to the reader by using the image of ticking and patches?

Answer choice A: Is the author trying to show the reader a sense of uniformity? The mother mends the family's torn clothing, but the colors of the patches are completely different than the material of the clothing. If you were to see their patched clothing, it would not seem uniform at all. This is not the best answer choice.

Answer choice B: Think about the family you've just read about. All of them, even the young boy, work, but they can't afford books or new clothing. Are they living in poverty? It seems that way. Odd-colored patches are sometimes a symbol of poverty. This seems like the best answer choice. However, you should always read all of the choices before making a decision.

Answer choice C: Are the ticking and patches a symbol of strength? They do make the clothes last longer, but they don't make them stronger. The patches do not seem to be a symbol of strength. You can eliminate this answer choice.

Answer choice D: When you read about the ticking and patches, did you think the family was experiencing hopelessness? Taking the time and effort to sew up damaged clothing seems to indicate hope. The family wants to make their belongings last longer, and they are willing to work hard for a better life. This is not the correct answer. Choice B is the best answer.

STEP TWO SIDEBAR INSTRUCTION

Read the selection and answer the questions that follow. Use the Sidebar Instruction to help you choose the correct answer.

Selection from Misery

by Anton Chekhov

Translated by Constance Garnett

1   *"To Whom Shall I Tell My Grief?"*

2   The twilight of evening. Big flakes of wet snow are whirling lazily about the street lamps, which have just been lighted, and lying in a thin soft layer on roofs, horses' backs, shoulders, caps. Iona Potapov, the sledge-driver*, is all white like a ghost. He sits on the box without stirring, bent as double as the living body can be bent. If a regular snowdrift fell on him it seems as though even then he would not think it necessary to shake it off. . . . His little mare is white and motionless too. Her stillness, the angularity of her lines, and the stick-like straightness of her legs make her look like a halfpenny gingerbread horse. She is probably lost in thought. Anyone who has been torn away from the plough, from the familiar gray landscapes, and cast into this slough, full of monstrous lights, of unceasing uproar and hurrying people, is bound to think.

3   It is a long time since Iona and his nag have budged. They came out of the yard before dinner-time and not a single fare yet. But now the shades of evening are falling on the town. The pale light of the street lamps changes to a vivid color, and the bustle of the street grows noisicr.

4   "Sledge to Vyborgskaya!" Iona hears. "Sledge!"

5   Iona starts, and through his snow-plastered eyelashes sees an officer in a military overcoat with a hood over his head.

6   "To Vyborgskaya," repeats the officer. "Are you asleep? To Vyborgskaya!"

7   In token of assent Iona gives a tug at the reins which sends cakes of snow flying from the horse's back and shoulders. The officer gets into the sledge. The sledge-driver clicks to the horse, cranes his neck like a swan, rises in his seat, and more from habit than necessity brandishes his whip. The mare cranes her neck, too, crooks her stick-like legs, and hesitatingly sets off. . . .

8   "Where are you shoving, you devil?" Iona immediately hears shouts from the dark mass shifting to and fro before him. "Where the devil are you going? Keep to the r-right!"

9   "You don't know how to drive! Keep to the right," says the officer angrily.

10   A coachman driving a carriage swears at him; a pedestrian crossing the road and brushing the horse's nose with his shoulder looks at him angrily and shakes the snow off his sleeve. Iona fidgets on the box as though he were sitting on thorns, jerks his elbows, and turns his eyes about like one possessed, as though he did not know where he was or why he was there.

11   "What rascals they all are!" says the officer jocosely. "They are simply doing their best to run up against you or fall under the horse's feet. They must be doing it on purpose."

12   Iona looks as his fare and moves his lips. . . . Apparently he means to say something, but nothing comes but a sniff.

13   "What?" inquires the officer.

14   Iona gives a wry smile, and straining his throat, brings out huskily: "My son. . . ., er. . . . my son died this week, sir."

15   "H'm! What did he die of?"

16   Iona turns his whole body round to his fare, and says:

17   "Who can tell! It must have been from fever. . . . He lay three days in the hospital and then he died. . . . God's will."

18   "Turn round, you devil!" comes out of the darkness. "Have you gone cracked, you old dog? Look where you are going!"

19   "Drive on! drive on!. . . ." says the officer. "We shan't get there till tomorrow going on like this. Hurry up!"

20   The sledge-driver cranes his neck again, rises in his seat, and with heavy grace swings his whip. Several times he looks round at the officer, but the latter keeps his eyes shut and is apparently disinclined to listen. Putting his fare down at Vyborgskaya, Iona stops by a restaurant, and again sits huddled up on the box. . . . Again the wet snow paints him and his horse white. One hour passes, and then another. . . .

21   Three young men, two tall and thin, one short and hunchbacked, come up, railing at each other and loudly stamping on the pavement with their galoshes.

22   "Cabby, to the Police Bridge!" the hunchback cries in a cracked voice. "The three of us, . . . twenty kopecks*!"

23   Iona tugs at the reins and clicks to his horse. Twenty kopecks is not a fair price, but he has no thoughts for that. Whether it is a rouble or whether it is five kopecks does not matter to him now so long as he has a fare. . . . The three young men, shoving each other and using bad language, go up to the sledge, and all three try to sit down at once. The question remains to be settled: Which are to sit down and which one is to stand? After a long altercation, ill-temper, and abuse, they come to the conclusion that the hunchback must stand because he is the shortest.

24   "Well, drive on," says the hunchback in his cracked voice, settling himself and breathing down Iona's neck. "Cut along! What a cap you've got, my friend! You wouldn't find a worse one in all Petersburg. . . ."

---

* sledge-driver – a sledge is a wagon designed to be used on snow and ice

* kopecks – 100 kopecks is equal to a ruble (or rouble). The ruble is the Russian monetary unit. In 2005, one U.S. dollar is equal to 28 rubles.

1 In paragraph 16, the author writes that Iona "turns his whole body round" in order to speak with the officer. What does this phrase suggest?

A. how stiff Iona's back is from waiting in the sledge

B. how recklessly Iona is driving

C. how eager Iona is to talk with the officer

D. how softly the officer speaks

Ⓐ   Ⓑ   Ⓒ   Ⓓ

SIDEBAR INSTRUCTION
Look back at paragraph 16 and read about Iona turning around to speak with the officer. What would cause Iona to turn all the way around in order to answer the officer's question?

Read the excerpt from paragraph 2 in the box below.

> Iona Potapov, the sledge-driver, is all white like a ghost. He sits on the box without stirring, bent as double as the living body can be bent. If a regular snowdrift fell on him it seems as though even then he would not think it necessary to shake it off. . . . His little mare is white and motionless too.

2 What is suggested by this description of Iona and his horse?

A. Iona and his horse seem as lifeless as snow.

B. Russian winters are difficult to survive.

C. Iona seems to be connected to the horse.

D. Iona is mourning his son.

SIDEBAR INSTRUCTION
This question asks you to read an excerpt from the story and decide what the author wants to convey. Carefully read the excerpt and think about the descriptions in it. What do you think about Iona and his horse after reading this?

3 In paragraph 10, it says that Iona "fidgets on the box as though he were sitting on thorns." How does this simile appeal to the senses?

A. It describes the anger that Iona feels towards the pedestrians.

B. It reveals how bothered Iona is with his inner sadness.

C. It shows how uncomfortable Iona is to be near the officer.

D. It illicits the pain Iona feels from riding so long in the sledge.

(A) (B) (C) (D)

SIDEBAR INSTRUCTION
The author chooses his words and figures of speech carefully in order to help the reader understand Iona's feelings. The simile is used to emphasize Iona's restlessness. Read the choices and decide how this simile appeals to the senses.

Read this excerpt from paragraph 2 in the box below. It refers to Iona's horse.

> She is probably lost in thought.
> Anyone who has been torn away from
> the plough, from the familiar gray
> landscapes, and cast into this slough,
> full of monstrous lights, of unceasing
> uproar and hurrying people, is bound
> to think.

 4 What is the effect of the personification used to describe Iona's horse?

A. It illustrates how the city is not a friendly place.

B. It makes Iona's burden seem greater than the horse's burden.

C. It makes the horse seem smarter than Iona.

D. It suggests to the reader that the horse is remarkable.

(A) (B) (C) (D)

SIDEBAR INSTRUCTION
To answer this question, read the excerpt very carefully. Although it is talking about the horse, it is using the horse to convey an idea about humans. What is this idea?

5 What do the pauses and hums of Iona's dialog say about Iona's mood?

A. Iona is excited about his job.

B. Iona is uninterested in his passengers.

C. Iona is distracted by his grief.

D. Iona is bored with his life.

Ⓐ Ⓑ Ⓒ Ⓓ

SIDEBAR INSTRUCTION

Many people speak with pauses and hums. Relate real-life information to the mood of Iona. How is he feeling, and how does that show in his speech?

6 Describe the mood of the selection using relevant and specific information.

_____

_____

_____

_____

_____

_____

_____

_____

_____

STEP THREE ON YOUR OWN

Read the selection. Then answer the questions that follow.

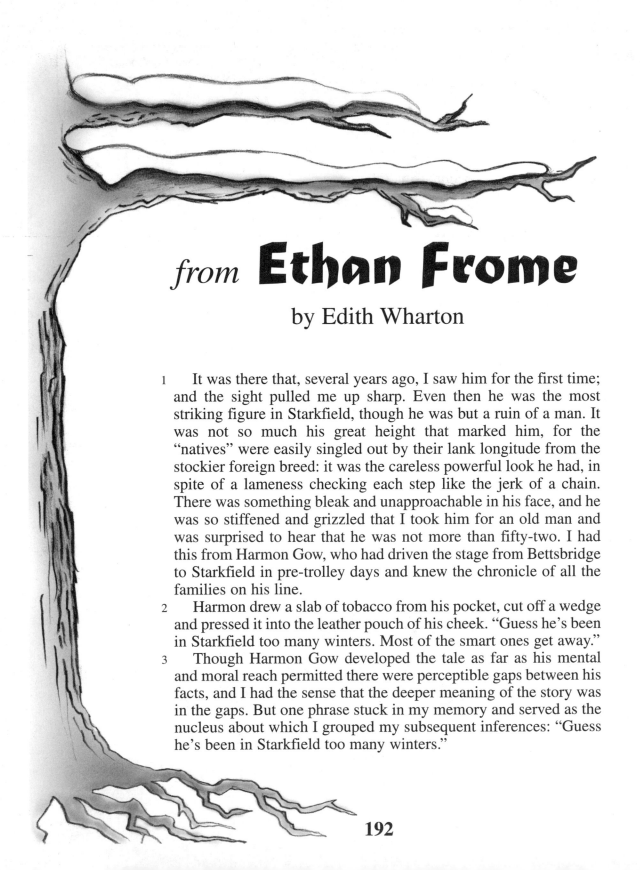

from Ethan Frome

by Edith Wharton

1   It was there that, several years ago, I saw him for the first time; and the sight pulled me up sharp. Even then he was the most striking figure in Starkfield, though he was but a ruin of a man. It was not so much his great height that marked him, for the "natives" were easily singled out by their lank longitude from the stockier foreign breed: it was the careless powerful look he had, in spite of a lameness checking each step like the jerk of a chain. There was something bleak and unapproachable in his face, and he was so stiffened and grizzled that I took him for an old man and was surprised to hear that he was not more than fifty-two. I had this from Harmon Gow, who had driven the stage from Bettsbridge to Starkfield in pre-trolley days and knew the chronicle of all the families on his line.

2   Harmon drew a slab of tobacco from his pocket, cut off a wedge and pressed it into the leather pouch of his cheek. "Guess he's been in Starkfield too many winters. Most of the smart ones get away."

3   Though Harmon Gow developed the tale as far as his mental and moral reach permitted there were perceptible gaps between his facts, and I had the sense that the deeper meaning of the story was in the gaps. But one phrase stuck in my memory and served as the nucleus about which I grouped my subsequent inferences: "Guess he's been in Starkfield too many winters."

192

4   Before my own time there was up I had learned to know what that meant. Yet I had come in the degenerate day of trolley, bicycle and rural delivery, when communication was easy between the scattered mountain villages, and the bigger towns in the valleys, such at Bettsbridge and Shadd's Falls, had libraries, theatres and Y.M.C.A. halls to which the youth of the hills could descend for recreation. But when winter shut down on Starkfield, and the village lay under a sheet of snow perpetually renewed from the pale skies, I began to see what life there—or rather its negation—must have been in Ethan Frome's young manhood.

5   I had been sent up by my employers on a job connected with the big power-house at Corbury Junction, and a long-drawn carpenters' strike had so delayed the work that I found myself anchored at Starkfield—the nearest habitable spot—for the best part of the winter. I chafed at first, and then, under the hypnotizing effect of routine, gradually began to find a grim satisfaction in the life. During the early part of my stay I had been struck by the contrast between the vitality of the climate and the deafness of the community. Day by day, after the December snows were over, a blazing blue sky poured down torrents of light and air on the white landscape, which gave them back in an intenser glitter. One would have supposed that such an atmosphere must quicken the emotions as well as the blood; but it seemed to produce no change except that of retarding still more the sluggish pulse of Starkfield. When I had been there a little longer, and had seen this phase of crystal clearness followed by long stretches of sunless cold; when the storms of February had pitched their white tents about the devoted village and the wild cavalry of March winds had charged down to their support, I began to understand why Starkfield emerged from its six months' siege like a starved garrison capitulating without quarter. Twenty years earlier the means of resistance must have been far fewer, and the enemy in command of almost all the lines of across the beleaguered villages; and, considering these things, I felt the sinister force of Harmon's phrase: "Most of the smart ones get away." But if that were the case, how could any combination of obstacles have hindered the flight of a man like Ethan Frome?

Read the author's description of winter in the box below.

> The winter weather is described as an attacking army.

7 What does this personification suggest?

A. Winter is cruel.

B. An attacking army is more successful in the winter.

C. An attacking army will be defeated in the winter.

D. Winter weather has the same effect as an attacking army.

Ⓐ Ⓑ Ⓒ Ⓓ

8 What word **best** describes the tone of this excerpt?

A. depressing

B. peaceful

C. cheerful

D. amusing

Ⓐ Ⓑ Ⓒ Ⓓ

Read Harmon Gow's comment on Ethan Frome in the box below.

> "Guess he's been in Starkfield too many winters. Most of the smart ones get away."

9 What does Gow's comment suggest about Frome?

A. Frome is smarter than the other residents of Starkfield.

B. Frome doesn't really live in Starkfield anymore.

C. Frome is probably not a smart man.

D. Gow remembers Frome from many years ago.

Ⓐ Ⓑ Ⓒ Ⓓ

10 Which of the following answers **best** describes the mood at the beginning of paragraph 4?

A. excitement over new knowledge of Ethan Frome

B. a feeling of disconnection from Starkfield's past

C. fear of Starkfield's brutal winters

D. pride in the development of the Starkfield community.

Ⓐ Ⓑ Ⓒ Ⓓ

Read the excerpt in the box below.

> "One would have supposed that such an atmosphere must quicken the emotions as well as the blood; but it seemed to produce no change except that of retarding still more the sluggish pulse of Starkfield."

11 What does this sentence mean?

A. The unusual weather in Starkfield was the pride and joy of its residents.

B. Starkfield's weather made its people even more depressed.

C. The people in Starkfield grew angry at each other in the winters.

D. People in Starkfield stopped reacting to the region's unusual weather.

Ⓐ Ⓑ Ⓒ Ⓓ

12 Using imagery from the passage, describe Ethan Frome.

_____

_____

_____

_____

_____

_____

_____

_____

LESSON 12

In addition to reading passages and answering questions about these passages, you will be given a writing prompt for which you will have to write out your answer. This prompt will be based on literature. It will ask you to remember something about a book or short story you have read. This prompt is based on the following standards:

Standard 19   Students will write compositions with a clear focus, logically related ideas to develop it, and adequate detail.

Standard 20   Students will select and use appropriate genres, modes of reasoning, and speaking styles when writing for different audiences and rhetorical purposes.

Standard 21   Students will demonstrate improvement in organization, content, paragraph development, level of detail, style, tone and word choice (diction) in their compositions after revising them.

Standard 22   Students will use knowledge of standard English conventions to edit their writing.

SAMPLE PROMPT

> Characters in books sometimes undergo a personality change as a result of an experience. They might become stronger after living through a tragic event or more open and honest after meeting someone special.
>
> From a work of literature you have read in or out of school, select a character who, in your opinion, has undergone a personality change. In a well-developed composition, identify that character and explain what happened to change him or her.

Before you can write an essay in response to this writing prompt, you have to think of a character in a book or a story that has undergone some kind of change. Remember some of the books and short stories you have read in school and at home. Think of a character who has undergone a change. After you do this, do a rough outline similar to the one below.

A character who has undergone a change is Santiago in Ernest Hemingway's *The Old Man and the Sea*.

- Santiago is elderly and feels useless.

- He does not catch many fish and loses his fishing partner.

- He pulls and struggles three days to catch a marlin.

- When he finally catches it, he feels good about his own strength.

- While he must sacrifice the prized fish to keep predators at bay, its skeleton creates a stir in the town where Santiago lives. Santiago is a stronger person as a result of the experience.

Once you have chosen a character and have a rough outline, write your essay. When you finish, check your essay for the following:

- Make sure you have responded correctly to the writing prompt.

- Check your organization. Make sure each of your paragraphs discusses one idea and that each paragraph has a topic sentence.

- Make sure your essay has an introduction and a conclusion.

- Check your grammar and spelling.

SIDEBAR PROMPT

Use the Sidebar Instruction to help you respond to the writing prompt below.

The setting is the time and place of a story. The setting might take place in a rural area many years ago. If it is science-fiction, it might take place in space in the future.

Select a work of literature you have read in or out of school. In a well-developed composition, discuss why the setting was important to the plot.

SIDEBAR INSTRUCTION

Begin by remembering a book or short story with a unique setting. Then jot down the role the setting played in the book. Ask yourself why the setting was an important part of the work of literature. Use the lines below to create a rough outline.

ON YOUR OWN PROMPT

Characters in literature often must make important decisions. They might have to choose what type of life they want to live. They might have to choose whether to live in a certain place or with a certain person.

From a work of literature you have read in or out of school, select a character who, in your opinion, made an important decision about his or her life. In a well-developed composition, identify that character and discuss the decision he or she made.

Organize your ideas here:

_____

_____

_____

_____

_____

_____

_____

_____

_____

_____

_____

_____

_____

_____

This section reviews the standards you have just learned. The questions in this review are for Standards 13, 15, 19, 20, 21, and 22.

Moving the Furniture Around

by Anna Quindlen

1   The man who wears an Army blanket and holds out a cardboard coffee cup in the Christopher Street subway station has a method to what some might call his madness. When he is told to leave the landing there, he goes two blocks down to the station from which trains run beneath the Hudson River to New Jersey. If that station is inhospitable, short on commuters or long on cops, he walks east to the West Fourth Street subway station. And he goes back to Chistopher Street if there are problems at West Fourth.

2   The subway has always been a good place to collect money. It is not uncommon to sit on a train and have the narrow tube filled with fund-raisers' speechifying: "Good afternoon, ladies and gentlemen. I represent the Sons of the Lord community outreach program in Brooklyn!" It is not unheard of to sit on a train and find your life on the line: "Give me your money or I'll cut you bad." The definition of captive audience is a dozen people on an express train between stations.

3   But the New York City Transit Authority had banned begging on the subway, and the Supreme Court last week let stand that ban. The legal pavane included pages of discussion of whether begging is speech or begging is behavior.

4   Once again, we've wasted time and money by dealing with the homeless backward. Too much energy has gone into deciding where we do not want them to be, and making sure that they would not be there. Benches were outfitted with dividers so that no one could lie down. Police were taught to turn people out of public buildings. And the Transit Authority rousted them

off trains. The exercise is reminiscent of moving furniture in a small apartment; you can put the couch in a number of places, but you cannot make it unobtrusive. The secret is to find a place where the couch fits.

5   There is no doubt that some of the homeless belong in psychiatric hospitals, but the number is probably much smaller than we believe. Mary Scullion, who runs two communal homes for women in Philadelphia, took a census five years ago of habitual street dwellers in Center City, identified by name and location 115 who appeared to be mentally ill, and set out to see if they were salvageable. Today, only five of them are in long-term psychiatric care. Eight are still on the streets. The rest are living in supervised residences or with their families.

6   Four years ago a woman named Ellen Baxter opened a single-room-occupancy building in upper Manhattan for homeless men and women. Today she is preparing to open her fifth building, a $4 million city-financed renovation that contains seventy-five studio apartments for individuals and seven two-bedroom apartments for families. None of the people in her buildings need to be in institutions, but few of them are ready to live without the assistance of the staff Columbia University provides, to help with their medical problems and their addictions, to negotiate the social service maze and what Ms. Baxter calls "the paperwork of poverty."

7   We can do much more of this, or we can continue to waste time and money moving these people around like so much furniture. One of the craziest ladies on the streets of Center City, a woman considered totally lost to normal life, lives in a group residence and works full time now, and Mary Scullion says that since that woman has been getting enough food and sleep and medical attention it's amazing, the resemblance she bears to you and me.

8   Discussions about the homeless always remind me of a woman who told me that she was damned if her tax dollars were going to pay for birth control for the poor. Come to think of it, she said, she didn't want her tax dollars paying for any social welfare programs. I wanted to say to her: If you don't pay for birth control, you'll have to pay for schools. If you don't pay for schools, you're going to pay for welfare. And if you don't pay for any of those things, you're going to spend a small fortune on prisons.

9   The question is not whether we will pay. It is what we want to pay for, and what works. The negative approach, the deciding where we want people to not be, has been a deplorable failure. There are those who believe the homeless are either criminal or crazy, that one way or another they should be locked up. It's worth remembering that it costs far more to lock someone up than to give them, as Ms. Scullion and Ms. Baxter have, a key of their own.

1 Which of the following words best expresses the narrator's mood throughout this passage?

A. disbelief

B. satisfaction

C. frustration

D. seriousness

Ⓐ Ⓑ Ⓒ Ⓓ

2 What example does the author give in paragraph 1 to illustrate the problem discussed in the essay?

A. She tells about a law banning begging on the subway.

B. She describes how a homeless man is pushed from place to place.

C. She shows how people feel about the homeless on subways.

D. She describes what it is like to have no place to live.

Ⓐ Ⓑ Ⓒ Ⓓ

Read the sentence from paragraph 4 in the box below.

> The exercise is reminiscent of moving furniture in a small apartment; you can put the couch in a number of places, but you cannot make it unobtrusive.

3 What does the "couch" metaphor emphasize?

A. that the homeless need a place where they belong

B. that the homeless feel awkward in any situation

C. that there are too many homeless people in New York

D. that there are not enough places where the homeless can go

Ⓐ Ⓑ Ⓒ Ⓓ

4 What does the author say in paragraph 7 to show that homeless people can be helped?

A. She compares a homeless woman to a piece of furniture.

B. She offers proof that most homeless people need food and medicine.

C. She discusses the successes of homeless people living in group homes.

D. She gives an example of a former homeless woman who now leads a normal life.

Ⓐ Ⓑ Ⓒ Ⓓ

5 What tone is set by the author in implying that the homeless are harmless? Support your answer with details and information from the passage.

_____

_____

_____

_____

_____

_____

_____

_____

_____

_____

6 What images does the author create of the homeless in "Men at Work"?
Use details and information from the passage to support your answer.

_____

_____

_____

_____

_____

_____

_____

_____

_____

_____

WRITING PROMPT

> Characters in books and short stories often share a special relationship with someone. A character might have a best friend who is very much alike or different from him or her. A character might also have a parent or child with whom he or she shares a special bond.
>
> From a work of literature you have read in or out of school, select two characters who, in your opinion, share a special bond. In a well-developed composition, identify these characters and discuss the bond they share.

Organize your ideas here:

_____

_____

_____

_____

_____

_____

_____

_____

_____

_____

_____

_____

Posttest

COMPOSITION

Sometimes literature can teach us important life lessons. In many novels and short stories, characters experience turning points in their lives that result in valuable lessons.

Select a work of literature you have read in or out of school that teaches a valuable lesson. In a well-developed composition, identify the lesson and explain why you think it was valuable.

Pages 208 and 209 are for the rough draft. The final copy should be written on pages 247 and 248 in your Student Answer Booklet.

_____

_____

_____

_____

_____

_____

_____

_____

_____

_____

_____

_____

_____

_____

_____

_____

_____

SESSION 1

DIRECTIONS

This session contains three reading selections with seventeen multiple-choice questions and two open-response questions. Mark your answers to these questions in the space provided in your Student Answer Booklet (page 249).

Excerpt from

A History of Aeronautics

by E. Charles Vivian

1   There was never a more enthusiastic and consistent student of the problems of flight than Otto Lilienthal, who was born in 1848 at Anklam, Pomerania, and even from his early school-days dreamed and planned the conquest of the air. His practical experiments began when, at the age of thirteen, he and his brother Gustav made wings consisting of wooden framework covered with linen, which Otto attached to his arms, and then ran downhill flapping them. In consequence of possible derision on the part of other boys, Otto confined these experiments for the most part to moonlit nights, and gained from them some idea of the resistance offered by flat surfaces to the air. It was in 1867 that the two brothers began really practical work, experimenting with wings which, from their design, indicate some knowledge of Besnier* and the history of his gliding experiments; these wings the brothers fastened to their backs, moving them with their legs after the fashion of one attempting to swim. Before they had achieved any real success in gliding the Franco-German war came as an interruption; both brothers served in this campaign, resuming their experiments in 1871 at the conclusion of hostilities.

2   The experiments made by the brothers previous to the war had convinced Otto that previous experimenters in gliding flight had failed through reliance on empirical conclusions* or else through incomplete observation on their own part, mostly of bird flight. . .

3   It was in the summer of 1891 that he built his first glider of rods of peeled willow, over which was stretched strong cotton fabric; with this, which had a supporting surface of about 100 square feet, Otto Lilienthal launched himself in the air from a springboard, making glides which, at first of only a few feet, gradually lengthened. As his experience of the supporting qualities of the air progressed he gradually altered his designs until, when Pilcher* visited him in the spring of 1895, he experimented with a glider, roughly made of peeled willow rods and cotton fabric, having an area of 150 square feet and weighing half a hundredweight.* By this time Lilienthal had moved from his springboard to a conical artificial hill which he had thrown up on level ground at Grosse Lichterfelde, near Berlin. This hill was made with earth taken from the excavations incurred in constructing a canal, and had a cave inside in which Lilienthal stored his machines. . .

4   Lilienthal's work did not end with simple gliding, though he did not live to achieve machine-driven flight. Having, as he considered, gained sufficient experience with gliders, he constructed a power-driven machine which weighed altogether about 90 lbs., and this was thoroughly tested. The extremities of its wings were made to flap, and the driving power was obtained from a cylinder of compressed carbonic acid gas, released through a hand-operated valve which, Lilienthal anticipated, would keep the machine in the air for four minutes. There were certain minor accidents to the mechanism, which delayed the trial flights, and on the day that Lilienthal had determined

to make his trial he made a long gliding flight. . . [H]e fell from a height of 50 feet, breaking his spine, and the next day he died.

5   It may be said that Lilienthal accomplished as much as any one of the great pioneers of flying. As brilliant in his conceptions as da Vinci* had been in his, and as conscientious a worker as Borelli, he laid the foundations on which Pilcher, Chanute, and Professor Montgomery were able to build to such good purpose. His book on bird flight, published in 1889, with the authorship credited both to Otto and his brother Gustav, is regarded as epoch-making; his gliding experiments are no less entitled to this description.

6. In England Lilienthal's work was carried on by Percy Sinclair Pilcher, who, born in 1866, completed six years' service in the British Navy by the time that he was nineteen, and then went through a course of engineering, subsequently joining [inventor Hiram] Maxim in his experimental work. It was not until 1895 that he began to build the first of the series of gliders with which he earned his place among the pioneers of flight...

7   It was in the spring of 1896 that Pilcher built his third glider, the "Gull," with 300 square feet of area and a weight of 55 lbs. The size of this machine rendered it unsuitable for experiment in any but very calm weather, and it incurred such damage when experiments were made in a breeze that Pilcher found it necessary to build a fourth, which he named the "Hawk.". . .

8   With this machine Pilcher made some twelve glides at Eynsford in Kent in the summer of 1896, and as he progressed he increased the length of his glides, and also handled the machine more easily, both in the air and in landing. He was occupied with plans for fitting an engine and propeller to the "Hawk," but, in these early days of the internal combustion engine, was unable to get one light enough for his purpose. There were rumours of an engine weighing 15 lbs. which gave 1 horse-power, and was reported

to be in existence in America, but it could not be traced.

9   In the spring of 1897 Pilcher took up his gliding experiments again, obtaining what was probably the best of his glides on June 19th, when he alighted after a perfectly balanced glide of over 250 yards in length, having crossed a valley at a considerable height. . .

10   . . . [O]n September 30th, 1899, at Stamford Hall, Market Harborough, Pilcher agreed to give a demonstration of gliding flight, but owing to the unfavourable weather he decided to postpone the trial of [a newer glider] and to experiment with the "Hawk," which was intended to rise from a level field, towed by a line passing over a tackle drawn by two horses. At the first trial the machine rose easily, but the tow-line snapped when it was well clear of the ground, and the glider descended, weighed down through being sodden with rain. Pilcher resolved on a second trial, in which the glider again rose easily to about thirty feet, when one of the guy wires of the tail broke, and the tail collapsed; the machine fell to the ground, turning over, and Pilcher was unconscious when he was freed from the wreckage.

11   Hopes were entertained of his recovery, but he died on Monday, October 2nd, 1899, aged only thirty-four. His work in the cause of flying lasted only four years, but in that time his actual accomplishments were sufficient to place his name beside that of Lilienthal, with whom he ranks as one of the greatest exponents of gliding flight.

---

* Besnier – a French locksmith who supposedly flew a glider in 1678.
* *reliance on empirical conclusions* – focusing only on their experiments
* Percy Sinclair Pilcher (1866-1899) – an English gliding pioneer.
* *half a hundredweight* – fifty pounds
* Leonardo da Vinci designed flying machines as far back as the 1400s.

1 What is the author trying to suggest by describing Lilienthal's childhood experiments in paragraph 1?

A. Lilienthal did not have time for gliding.

B. Lilienthal was fascinated with flight.

C. Gliding was difficult in Lilienthal's era.

D. Gliding was common in Lilienthal's era.

2 What does the author mean by the statement in paragraph 11 that Pilcher's "accomplishments were sufficient to place his name beside that of Lilienthal"?

A. Pilcher and Lilienthal lived during the same time.

B. Pilcher and Lilienthal had always worked together.

C. Pilcher's work was as important as Lilienthal's.

D. Pilcher was highly respected by Lilienthal.

3 The excerpt from "A History of Aeronautics" can best be classified as

A. a narrative.

B. autobiographical.

C. journal writing.

D. expository writing.

4 Overall, the author's main point in writing this article was to

A. summarize the accomplishments of two early glider pilots.

B. inform readers of the tragic results of early flight attempts.

C. examine Otto Lilienthal's service in the Franco-German war.

D. educate readers about the theories of flight.

5 Which was the main reason why Pilcher did not install an engine on his glider?

A. He could not find a strong enough engine.

B. He could not find a light enough engine.

C. His best glider was damaged in a crash.

D. Engines were difficult to find in England.

6 In paragraph 5, the author writes that Lilienthal's work is "regarded as epoch-making." What does the author mean by this term?

A. He worked to build new machines.

B. He worked to improve existing machines.

C. His work was so great it changed history.

D. His work has not impacted the world.

7 Lilienthal flew his glider at night to avoid *derision* from other boys. This means that the boys would have

   A. ridiculed his experiments.

   B. destroyed his experiments.

   C. told adults about his gliders.

   D. insisted on flying his gliders.

8 In paragraph 2, we learn that Lilienthal believed other experimenters failed because they did not observe birds. This helps the reader conclude that Lilienthal

   A. felt that observing birds was useless.

   B. had a low opinion of other experimenters.

   C. wanted to know if gliding was natural.

   D. based his glider designs on bird wings.

Write your answer to open-response question 9 in the space provided in your Student Answer Booklet.

9 In the excerpt, the author describes Lilienthal's ideas, experiments, and accomplishments. Identify at least **three** character traits that Lilienthal demonstrated. Use relevant and specific information from the excerpt to support your answer.

Jules Verne's famous 1873 novel Around the World in Eighty Days *is a fictional account of Phileas Fogg, an English gentleman who decides to travel around the entire planet in under three months. In 1873 that was an unbelievable fantasy! With his sidekick, Passepartout, Fogg navigates through exotic locations and dangerous obstacles in pursuit of his goal.*

In this selection, Fogg and Passepartout meet for the first time.

from
Around the World in Eighty Days
by Jules Verne

1   "Faith," muttered Passepartout, somewhat flurried, "I've seen people at Madame Tussaud's as lively as my new master!"

2   Madame Tussaud's 'people', let it be said, are of wax, and are much visited in London; speech is all that is wanting to make them human.

3   During his brief interview with Mr Fogg, Passepartout had been carefully observing him. He appeared to be a man about forty years of age, with fine, handsome features, and a tall, well-shaped figure; his hair and whiskers were light, his forehead compact and unwrinkled, his face rather pale, his teeth magnificent. His countenance possessed in the highest degree what physiognomists* call 'repose in action', a quality of those who act rather than talk. Calm and phlegmatic, with a clear eye, Mr Fogg seemed a perfect type of that English composure which Angelica Kauffmann has so skillfully represented on canvas. Seen in the various phases of his daily life, he gave the idea of being perfectly well-balanced, as exactly regulated as a Leroy chronometer*. Phileas Fogg was, indeed, exactitude personified, and this was

betrayed even in the expression of his very hands and feet; for in men, as well as in animals, the limbs themselves are expressive of the passions.

4   He was so exact that he was never in a hurry, was always ready, and was economical alike of his steps and his motions. He never took one step too many, and always went to his destination by the shortest cut; he made no superfluous gestures, and was never seen to be moved or agitated. He was the most deliberate person in the world, yet always reached his destination at the exact moment.

5   He lived alone, and so to speak, outside of every social relation; and as he knew that in this world account must be taken of friction, and that friction retards, he never rubbed against anybody.

6   As for Passepartout, he was a true Parisian of Paris. Since he had abandoned his own country for England, taking service as a valet, he had in vain searched for a master after his own heart. Passepartout was by no means one of those pert dunces depicted by Molière, with a bold gaze and a nose held high in the air; he was an honest fellow, with a pleasant face, lips a trifle protruding, soft-mannered and serviceable, with a good round head such as one likes to see on the shoulders of a friend. His eyes were blue, his complexion rubicund,* his figure almost portly and well-built, his body muscular, and his physical powers fully developed by the exercises of his younger days. His brown hair was somewhat tumbled; for while the ancient sculptors are said to have known eighteen methods of arranging Minerva's tresses, Passepartout was familiar with but one of dressing his own: three strokes of a large-tooth comb completed his toilet*.

7   It would be rash to predict how Passepartout's lively nature would agree with Mr Fogg

---

*physiognomists – scientists who attempt to determine a
 person's character by studying that person's facial features
*chronometer – a precise clock
*rubicund – a healthy reddish complexion
*toilet – a routine of grooming

10 Given the information in this passage about Madame Tussaud, what business would she be most likely operate?

A. a physiognomy lab

B. a wax-statue museum

C. a painters' gallery

D. a chronometer factory

Read the excerpt from paragraph 4 in the box below. It refers to Mr. Fogg.

> He was the most deliberate person in the world . . .

11 What figure of speech is being used in the above excerpt?

A. hyperbole

B. simile

C. oxymoron

D. pun

12 According to the information about Passepartout, what words would best describe his character?

A. exact and deliberate

B. scheming and bitter

C. placid and quiet

D. energetic and outgoing

Read the sentence about Fogg from paragraph 5 in the box below.

> He lived alone, and so to speak, outside of every social relation; and as he knew that in this world account must be taken of friction, and that friction retards, he never rubbed against anybody.

13 This sentence is written to emphasize what idea?

A. Fogg had a quick temper and often got in fights.

B. Fogg was a solitary, introverted person.

C. Fogg was always on the run.

D. Fogg was making his behaviors known to Passepartout.

14 Which of the following **best** describes the writing style in this passage?

A. dialogue

B. editorializing

C. characterization

D. suspense

Poet Claude McKay was born in Jamaica, West Indies, in 1889. During his career, he wrote on a broad range of topics from racism to romance to his happy childhood in Jamaica. His poetry, characterized by passion and energy, helped inspire the Harlem Renaissance. As you read this poem, think about a place where you love to be. Use information from the poem to answer the questions that follow.

After the Winter

by Claude McKay

1 Some day, when trees have shed their leaves,
    And against the morning's white
The shivering birds beneath the eaves
    Have sheltered for the night,
5 We'll turn our faces southward, love,
    Toward the summer isle
Where bamboos spire to shafted grove
    And wide-mouthed orchids smile.

And we will seek the quiet hill
10   Where towers the cotton tree,
And leaps the laughing crystal rill*,
    And works the droning bee.
And we will build a cottage there
    Beside an open glade,
15 With black-ribbed blue-bells blowing near,
    And ferns that never fade.

---

* rill – a small body of water; a creek

15 In line 5, what does "turn our faces southward" suggest?

A. They will try to remember warm summer days.

B. They will travel south where it is warmer.

C. They will turn their faces toward the sun.

D. They will gather warmth from the sun.

16 Which extremes are contrasted in the first stanza?

A. winter and summer

B. hate and love

C. light and dark

D. male and female

17 Which word best describes the mood in the second stanza?

A. suspenseful

B. nostalgic

C. melancholy

D. euphoric

18 In line 15, the sound repetition in "black-ribbed blue-bells blowing" is an example of

A. harmony.

B. alliteration.

C. assonance.

D. onomatopoeia.

Write your answer to open-response question 19 in the space provided in your Student Answer Booklet.

19 In the poem "After the Winter," the author frequently uses imagery to create mood. Identify at least **three** examples of imagery that convey mood in the second stanza of the poem. Use relevant and specific information from the poem to support your answer.

SESSION 2

DIRECTIONS

This session contains one reading selection with seven multiple-choice questions and one open-response question. Mark your answers to these question in the space provided in your Student Answer Booklet (page 251).

Benjamin Franklin, one of the most important figures in United States history, was also one of its busiest. He was a statesman, publisher, scientist, inventor, and writer! More than 200 years after his death, people still have difficulty believing how much he accomplished. In Franklin's autobiography, he sheds light on the events of his early life that led to his great achievements. Here, Franklin reflects on his years as a working teenager.

Excerpt from
The Autobiography of Benjamin Franklin

"Writing Little Pieces for This Paper. . ."

1   My brother had in 1720 or 1721 begun to print a newspaper. It was the second that appeared in America, and was called the *New England Courant*. The only one before it was the *Boston News-Letter*. I remember his being dissuaded by some of his friends from the undertaking, as not likely to succeed, one newspaper being, in their judgment, enough for America. At this time (1771) there are not less than five-and-twenty. He went on, however, with the undertaking, and after having worked in composing the types and printing off the sheets, I was employed to carry the papers through the streets to the customers.

2   He had some ingenious men among his friends who amused themselves by writing little pieces for this paper, which gained it credit and made it more in demand, and these gentlemen often visited us. Hearing their conversations and their accounts of the approbation* their papers were received with, I was excited to try my hand among them; but, being still a boy and suspecting that my brother would object to printing anything of mine in his paper if he knew it to be mine, I contrived to disguise my hand, and, writing an anonymous paper, I put it in at night under the door of the

221

printing-house. It was found in the morning, and communicated to his writing friends when they called in as usual. They read it, commented on it in my hearing, and I had the exquisite pleasure of finding it met with their approbation and that in their different guesses at the author, none were named but men of some character among us for learning and ingenuity. I suppose now that I was rather lucky in my judges and that perhaps they were not really so very good ones as I then esteemed them.

3   Encouraged, however, by this, I wrote and conveyed in the same way to the press several more papers which were equally approved; and I kept my secret till my small fund of sense for such performances was pretty well exhausted and then I discovered* it, when I began to be considered a little more by my brother's acquaintance, and in a manner that did not quite please him, as he thought, probably with reason, that it tended to make me too vain. And, perhaps, this might be one occasion of the differences that

we began to have about this time. Though a brother, he considered himself as my master and me as his apprentice and accordingly, expected the same services from me as he would from another, while I thought he demeaned me too much in some he required of me, who from a brother expected more indulgence. Our disputes were often brought before our father, and I fancy I was either generally in the right or else a better pleader, because the judgment was generally in my favor. But my brother was passionate, and had often beaten me, which I took extremely amiss; and, thinking my apprenticeship very tedious, I was continually wishing for some opportunity of shortening it, which at length offered in a manner unexpected.

4   (I fancy his harsh and tyrannical treatment of me might be a means of impressing me with that aversion to arbitrary power that has stuck to me through my whole life.)

5   One of the pieces in our newspaper on some political point, which I have now forgotten, gave offense to the Assembly. He was taken up, censured, and imprisoned for a month, by the speaker's warrant, I suppose because he would not discover his author. I, too, was taken up and examined before the Council; but, though I did not give them any satisfaction, they contented themselves with admonishing me, and dismissed me, considering me, perhaps, as an apprentice who was bound to keep his master's secrets.

6   During my brother's confinement, which I resented a good deal, notwithstanding our private differences, I had the management of the paper; and I made bold to give our rulers some rubs in it, which my brother took very kindly, while others began to consider me in an unfavorable light, as a young genius that had a turn for libeling* and satire. My brother's discharge was accompanied with an order of the House (a very odd one), that "James Franklin should no longer print the paper called the *New England Courant.*"

7   There was a consultation held in our printing-house among his friends, what

222

he should do in this case. Some proposed to evade the order by changing the name of the paper; but my brother, seeing inconveniences in that, it was finally concluded on as a better way to let it be printed for the future under the name of BENJAMIN FRANKLIN; and to avoid the censure of the Assembly, that might fall on him as still printing it by his apprentice, the contrivance was that my old indenture* should be returned to me with a full discharge on the back of it to be shown on occasion, but to secure to him the benefit of my service I was to sign new indentures for the remainder of the term, which were to be kept private. A very flimsy scheme it was; however, it was immediately executed, and the paper went on accordingly under my name for several months.

"I Took Upon Me to Assert My Freedom..."

8   At length, a fresh difference arising between my brother and me, I took upon me to assert my freedom, presuming that he would not venture to produce the new indentures. It was not fair in me to take this advantage, and this I therefore reckon one of the first errata* of my life; but the unfairness of it weighed little with me when under the impressions of resentment for the blows his passion too often urged him to bestow upon me, though he was otherwise not an ill-natured man: perhaps I was too saucy and provoking.

9   When he found I would leave him, he took care to prevent my getting employment in any other printing-house of the town by going round and speaking to every master, who accordingly refused to give me work. I then thought of going to New York as the nearest place where there was a printer; and I was rather inclined to leave Boston when I reflected that I had already made myself a little obnoxious to the governing party, and, from the arbitrary proceedings of the Assembly in my brother's case, it was likely I might if I stayed soon bring myself into scrapes; and farther, that my indiscreet disputations* about religion began to make me pointed at with horror by good people as an infidel or atheist. I determined on the point, but my father now siding with my brother, I was sensible that if I attempted to go openly, means would be used to prevent me. My friend Collins, therefore, undertook to manage a little for me. He agreed with the captain of a New York sloop* for my passage under the notion of my being a young acquaintance of his that had got a naughty girl with child, whose friends would compel me to marry her and therefore I could not appear or come away publicly. So I sold some of my books to raise a little money, was taken on board privately, and as we had a fair wind, in three days I found myself in New York, near 300 miles from home, a boy of but seventeen, without the least recommendation to or knowledge of any person in the place, and with very little money in my pocket."

---

*approbation – praise
*discovered – in this excerpt, Franklin uses 'discover'
 to mean 'reveal'
*libeling – telling damaging lies
*indenture – a contract to do a certain job
*errata – a list of errors in printing
*indiscreet disputations – obvious debates
*sloop – a sailing boat

20 According to this excerpt, which describes Franklin's **first** duty at his job?

    A. "carry the papers through the streets to the customers"

    B. "writing little pieces for this paper"

    C. "sold some of my books to raise a little money"

    D. "writing an anonymous paper"

21 In paragaph 4, what does *aversion* mean?

    A. indulgence

    B. dislike

    C. enjoyment

    D. undertaking

22 According to the article, how did Benjamin Franklin's brother James avoid punishment from the Assembly?

    A. James ended his newspaper immediately.

    B. James printed his paper under Benjamin's name.

    C. James changed the paper's name to *New England Courant*.

    D. James changed the paper's name to *Boston News-Letter*.

Read the sentence from the excerpt in the box below:

> At length, a fresh difference arising between my brother and me, I took upon me to not venture to produce the new indentures. It was not fair in me to take this advantage, and this I therefore reckon one of the first errata of my life . . .

23 Which statement best describes Franklin's memories of his decision?

    A. Franklin considered his motivations unjust.

    B. Franklin was not sure what had motivated him to act as he did.

    C. Franklin was relieved that he'd chosen to leave his brother behind.

    D. Franklin considered the results of his actions life-changing.

24 According to paragraph 9, why did Franklin choose to go to New York?

    A. Franklin had fathered a child in Boston but didn't want to get married.

    B. Franklin had upset the leaders in Boston.

    C. Franklin's father forced him to move far away.

    D. Franklin thought a printer in New York might hire him.

25 What does *anonymous* mean in paragraph 2?

    A. signed

    B. unidentified

    C. identified

    D. uninformed

26 In the excerpt, paragraph 4 is mostly an example of which literary style?

    A. an oxymoron

    B. an aside

    C. a metaphor

    D. a pun

Write your answer to open-response question 27 in the space provided in your Student Answer Booklet.

27 In this essay, Benjamin Franklin describes a terrible conflict he experienced with his brother. What was the conflict and how and when did it begin? Use details and information from the essay in your answer.

SESSION 3

DIRECTIONS

This session contains two reading selections with twelve multiple-choice questions and one open-response question. Mark your answers to these questions in the spaces provided in your Student Answer Booklet (page 252).

One of nature's strongest and most unstoppable forces, the hurricane, is a major problem in many parts of the world today. Hurricanes have plagued humans for thousands of years—and may have even influenced the extinction of the dinosaurs millions of years before humans. Read this article to learn about some of the ways hurricanes have changed the course of history.

Excerpt from
Hurricanes of History–
from Dinosaur Times to Today

by Willie Drye

1   As storm season looms, explore the historic mayhem wrought by hurricanes. For millennia, it seems, almost nothing has been safe from these summer tempests—not World War II warships, not treasure-filled galleons, perhaps not even the dinosaurs.

2   More than 400 years ago explorer Tristan de Luna had some ambitious plans—he was going to establish the first permanent Spanish settlement in a land called Florida, and use this base to explore North America and spread the Christian religion.

3   In June 1559 de Luna and 1,500 colonists, soldiers, and friars boarded a dozen ships in Veracruz, Mexico, expecting to reach their destination in two weeks. But it was a raucous* summer on the Gulf of Mexico, and for two months storms blew de Luna's fleet back and forth across the water.

4   In mid-August, the sea-weary settlers finally landed near what is now Pensacola. Most of their food was gone, and many of their horses had been killed in the long, tempestuous crossing.

5   Still, de Luna tried to remain optimistic, believing he'd landed at one of the world's best natural harbors. But only a few weeks later, a hurricane roared off the Gulf and smashed into de Luna's bedraggled settlement, killing hundreds and destroying nine ships.

6   Spain's King Phillip decided he'd had enough of the storm-battered Gulf Coast. He

226

ordered de Luna to send an expedition to start a settlement on Florida's east coast.

7   Another hurricane sank this tiny fleet soon after it departed, however, and in 1561 Spain evacuated de Luna's surviving colonists.

8   De Luna's ill-fated colony was among the earliest recorded examples of how hurricanes have altered history, but the powerful summer storms have been influencing the course of events for perhaps millions of years.

9   Sailors from Christopher Columbus to World War II admirals have had to contend with hurricanes. The storms have intervened in naval battles, spilled immense riches into the sea, shattered the grandiose dreams of real estate developers, and caused headaches for politicians. And they may have helped exterminate the dinosaurs.

Did Hurricanes Do In the Dinosaurs?

10   No humans were around to make permanent records of prehistoric hurricanes. But Kerry Emanuel, professor of meteorology at the Massachusetts Institute of Technology, thinks conditions may have existed about 65 million years ago that could have spawned prehistoric hypercanes far more powerful than modern storms.

11   Scientists have long thought that the dinosaurs may have died after an asteroid struck the Earth and caused dramatic climate changes. Emanuel and other researchers think the asteroid could have heated the ancient oceans to as much as 50 degrees Celsius (about 120 degrees Fahrenheit).

12   Hurricanes draw their immense energy from warm ocean water, and this superheated water could have fueled storms with winds exceeding 700 miles (1,130 kilometers) an hour.

13   These prehistoric monster hurricanes could have carried water vapor high into the stratosphere, causing lethal changes on our planet that would have doomed the dinosaurs.

14   Emanuel adds, however, that his concept of hypercanes is only a theory and he hasn't figured out a way to test it.

15   Researchers have discovered clues from more recent hurricanes dating back only a few thousand years.

16   Kam-biu Liu, a geology professor at Louisiana State University, discovered ocean sand in core samples from inland lakes on the coast of the Gulf of Mexico. From these samples, Liu concluded that extremely powerful hurricanes battered the Gulf Coast and dumped the sand into the lakes.

17   Liu thinks the core samples indicate that hurricanes that would be considered catastrophic by modern standards were regularly battering the Gulf Coast thousands of years ago.

18   From about 3,400 years ago to about 1,000 years ago, the Gulf Coast was hit repeatedly by very powerful hurricanes, Liu said. The frequency of hits increases by three to five times more than today.

19   The ancient Maya Indians—who had their heyday* in Mexico and Central America from about A.D. 250 to 900—had more than a passing familiarity with the tempests that regularly howled off the Atlantic. They called their god of storms Hurukan, and its likely that our term for the storms evolved from this name.

Storm-Sunk Treasure

20   Christopher Columbus somehow avoided the worst hurricanes at sea during his trans-Atlantic voyages of the 1490s, but he learned to respect the storms and recognize the conditions that occur when a hurricane is forming.

21   Columbus made a summer crossing in 1502. At Santo Domingo in what is now the Dominican Republic, he advised Spanish admirals that they'd be wise to postpone the departure of a fleet of treasure ships bound for Spain.

22   The admirals sneered at Columbus's warning and sailed straight into the teeth of a hurricane, losing more than two dozen ships, hundreds of lives, and a fortune in gold.

23   Spanish ventures in the New World were bedeviled by hurricanes in the 17th and 18th centuries.

24   In late July 1715 a fleet of 11 Spanish ships left Havana, Cuba. They were carrying gold and silver worth more than $300 million in today's U.S. dollars. Fleet commanders knew they were going to sea in the middle of the hurricane season, but Spain was desperate for cash after years of warfare.

25   On July 30 a killer hurricane caught the treasure fleet off Florida, smashing the ships and scattering them along the coast from Cape Canaveral to present-day Fort Pierce. More than a thousand people died, and Spain's badly needed treasure ended up on the bottom of the ocean.

---

*raucous – disorderly

*heyday – time of great success

28 The **main** purpose of this article is to

A. explain ways hurricanes have altered history.

B. describe the natural forces that cause hurricanes.

C. convince readers that hurricanes destroyed the dinosaurs.

D. teach readers about important events in history.

29 In paragraph 16, it says that Professor Kam-biu Liu found ocean sand in lakes. What theory was drawn from this discovery?

A. The lakes had once been connected to the ocean.

B. People or animals had transported ocean water to the lakes.

C. Hurricanes had dropped ocean water into the lakes.

D. Hurricanes had separated the lakes from the ocean.

30 According to this article, where does the term *hurricane* most likely come from?

A. The name of a city in Wisconsin: *Horicon*.

B. The name of a type of Japanese writing: *hiragana*.

C. The name of an ancient Asian country: *Hyrcania*.

D. The name of the Maya Indians' god of storms: *Hurukan*.

31 Paragraph 2 states that Tristan de Luna had hoped to start a Spanish settlement in "a land called Florida." What idea is the author most likely trying to convey with the term *a land called Florida*?

A. De Luna was not a good geographer.

B. De Luna had a very poor chance of succeeding in his journey.

C. Florida was a distant place about which little was known.

D. Florida was once an island.

32 In paragraph 23, the word *bedeviled* means

A. assisted

B. uncovered

C. rushed along

D. tormented

In paragraph 22, what figure of speech is the term *teeth of a hurricane*?

A. personification

B. simile

C. metaphor

D. characterization

 In paragraph 4, the word *tempestuous* means

A. argumentative

B. exhausting

C. stormy

D. caustic

Read this sentence from paragraph 11 in the box below.

> Emanuel and other researchers think the asteroid could have heated the ancient oceans to as much as 50 degrees Celsius (about 120 degrees Fahrenheit.)

 In the context of the article, the author uses this theory to support what point?

A. The heating of the water may have been caused by hurricanes.

B. The hot water may have fueled gigantic hurricanes.

C. The oceans may have evaporated and left behind salt.

D. The water may have become too hot to drink.

Write your answer to open-response question 36 in the space provided in your Student Answer Booklet.

 This article mentions a type of storm called a hypercane. Why does the author discuss hypercanes? How might hypercanes be related to the extinction of the dinosaurs? Use details and information from the article in your answer.

Susan Glaspell's Trifles *is a play about a murder mystery that brings to light some differences between men and women. The male investigators' wives examine the small details of Mrs. Wright's life. Read this excerpt to learn how the women piece together the story of Mrs. Wright.*

excerpt from
TRIFLES
by Susan Glaspell

1   **MRS: PETERS:** (*glancing around.*) Seems funny to think of a bird here. But she must have had one, or why should she have a cage? I wonder what happened to it.

MRS. HALE: I s'pose maybe the cat got it.

5   **MRS. PETERS:** No, she didn't have a cat. She's got that feeling some people have about cats—being afraid of them. My cat got in her room, and she was real upset and asked me to take it out.

MRS. HALE: My sister Bessie was like that. Queer, ain't it?

MRS. PETERS: (*examining the cage.*) Why, look at this door. It's
10   broke. One hinge is pulled apart.

MRS. HALE: (*looking, too.*) Looks as if someone must have been rough with it.

MRS. PETERS: Why, yes. (*She brings the cage forward and puts it on the table.*)

15   **MRS. HALE:** I wish if they're going to find any evidence they'd be about it. I don't like this place.

MRS. PETERS: But I'm awful glad you came with me, Mrs. Hale. It would be lonesome for me sitting here alone.

MRS. HALE: It would, wouldn't it? (*dropping her sewing.*) But I tell
20   you what I do wish, Mrs. Peters. I wish I had come over sometimes when she was here. I— (*looking around the room.*)—wish I had.

MRS. PETERS: But of course you were awful busy, Mrs. Hale—your house and your children.

MRS. HALE: I could've come. I stayed away because it weren't
25   cheerful—and that's why I ought to have come. I—I've never liked this place. Maybe because it's down in a hollow, and you don't see the road. I dunno what it is, but it's a lonesome place and always was. I wish I had come over to see Minnie Foster* sometimes. I can see now—
(*shakes her head.*)

30   **MRS. PETERS:**   Well, you mustn't reproach yourself, Mrs. Hale. Somehow we just don't see how it is with other folks until—something comes up.

MRS. HALE: Not having children makes less work—but it makes a quiet house, and Wright out to work all day, and no company when he
35   did come in. Did you know John Wright, Mrs. Peters?

MRS. PETERS: Not to know him; I've seen him in town. They say he was a good man.

MRS. HALE: Yes—good; he didn't drink, and kept his word as well as most, I guess, and paid his debts. But he was a hard man, Mrs. Peters.
40   Just to pass the time of day with him—(*shivers.*) Like a raw wind that gets to the bone. (pauses, her eye falling on the cage.) I should think she would 'a wanted a bird. But what do you suppose went with it?

MRS. PETERS: I don't know, unless it got sick and died. (*She reaches over and swings the broken door, swings it again, both women watch it.*)

45   **MRS. HALE:**   You weren't raised round here, were you? (*Mrs. Peters shakes her head.*) You didn't know—her?

MRS. PETERS: Not till they brought her yesterday.

MRS. HALE: She—come to think of it, she was kind of like a bird herself—real sweet and pretty, but kind of timid and—fluttery. How—
50   she—did—change. (*silence; then as if struck by a happy thought and relieved to get back to every day things.*) Tell you what, Mrs. Peters, why don't you take the quilt in with you? It might take up her mind.

MRS. PETERS: Why, I think that's a real nice idea, Mrs. Hale. There couldn't possibly be any objection to it, could there? Now, just what
55   would I take? I wonder if her patches are in here—and her things.
(*They look in the sewing basket.*)

MRS. HALE: Here's some red. I expect this has got sewing things in it (*brings out a fancy box.*) What a pretty box. Looks like something somebody would give you. Maybe her scissors are in here. (*Opens box.*
60   *Suddenly puts her hand to her nose.*) Why— (*Mrs. Peters bend nearer, then turns her face away.*) There's something wrapped up in this piece of silk.

MRS. PETERS: Why, this isn't her scissors.

MRS. HALE: (*lifting the silk.*) Oh, Mrs. Peters—it's— (*Mrs. Peters bend closer.*)

65   **MRS. PETERS:**   It's the bird.

---

*Minnie Foster is Mrs. Wright's maiden name.

37 Which word best describes the behavior of Mrs. Hale and Mrs. Peters?

   A. oppressive

   B. sneaky

   C. intrusive

   D. inconsistent

38 According to the excerpt, what was Mrs. Hale's regret?

   A. Mrs. Hale had wanted to marry Mr. Wright.

   B. Mrs. Hale regretted marrying Mr. Hale.

   C. Mrs. Hale regretted not visiting Mrs. Wright.

   D. Mrs. Hale regretted not visiting Mrs. Peters.

39 Mrs. Hale's suggestion that the Wrights' cat ate the bird was an example of

   A. conjecture.

   B. simile.

   C. derivation.

   D. testimony.

Read the line from the excerpt in the box below.

> **MRS. HALE:** Not having children makes less work—but it makes a quiet house, and Wright out to work all day, and no company when he did come in.

40 What point was Mrs. Hale trying to make with her statement?

   A. She thinks Mrs. Wright should have kept more pets.

   B. She thinks Mr. Wright's hard work was not appreciated.

   C. She is envious of the peace and quiet Mrs. Wright enjoyed.

   D. She thinks Mrs. Wright had a lonely and unfulfilling life.

Pretest Student
Answer Booklet

GRADE 10
English Language Arts

COMPOSITION

PRETEST ANSWER BOOKLET

Student's Name:		
LAST	FIRST	MI

School: _____ Teacher: _____

Female ○   Male ○   Grade ⑨ ⑩ ⑪ ⑫

1 Ⓐ Ⓑ Ⓒ Ⓓ

2 Ⓐ Ⓑ Ⓒ Ⓓ

3 Ⓐ Ⓑ Ⓒ Ⓓ

4 Ⓐ Ⓑ Ⓒ Ⓓ

5 Ⓐ Ⓑ Ⓒ Ⓓ

6 Ⓐ Ⓑ Ⓒ Ⓓ

7 Ⓐ Ⓑ Ⓒ Ⓓ

8 Ⓐ Ⓑ Ⓒ Ⓓ

9 In his inaugural address, Kennedy used motivational language to encourage citizens to take action that would make the country and the world a better place. Identify at least three such examples and explain how each one was motivational. Use relevant and specific information from the article to support your answer.

_____

_____

_____

_____

_____

_____

_____

_____

_____

10 Ⓐ Ⓑ Ⓒ Ⓓ

11 Ⓐ Ⓑ Ⓒ Ⓓ

12 Ⓐ Ⓑ Ⓒ Ⓓ

13 Ⓐ Ⓑ Ⓒ Ⓓ

14 Ⓐ Ⓑ Ⓒ Ⓓ

15 Ⓐ Ⓑ Ⓒ Ⓓ

16 Ⓐ Ⓑ Ⓒ Ⓓ

17 Ⓐ Ⓑ Ⓒ Ⓓ

18 Ⓐ Ⓑ Ⓒ Ⓓ

19 Explain why "A Birthday" is an appropriate title for Christina G. Rossetti's poem. Use relevant and specific information from this poem to support your answer.

_____

_____

_____

_____

_____

_____

_____

_____

_____

_____

_____

_____

_____

20 Ⓐ Ⓑ Ⓒ Ⓓ

21 Ⓐ Ⓑ Ⓒ Ⓓ

22 Ⓐ Ⓑ Ⓒ Ⓓ

23 Ⓐ Ⓑ Ⓒ Ⓓ

24 Ⓐ Ⓑ Ⓒ Ⓓ

25 Ⓐ Ⓑ Ⓒ Ⓓ

26 Ⓐ Ⓑ Ⓒ Ⓓ

27 Using information from the excerpt, what is the narrator's opinion of Jim Burden?

_____

_____

_____

_____

_____

_____

_____

_____

_____

_____

_____

_____

_____

_____

_____

28 Ⓐ Ⓑ Ⓒ Ⓓ   **32** Ⓐ Ⓑ Ⓒ Ⓓ

29 Ⓐ Ⓑ Ⓒ Ⓓ   **33** Ⓐ Ⓑ Ⓒ Ⓓ

30 Ⓐ Ⓑ Ⓒ Ⓓ   **34** Ⓐ Ⓑ Ⓒ Ⓓ

31 Ⓐ Ⓑ Ⓒ Ⓓ   **35** Ⓐ Ⓑ Ⓒ Ⓓ

36 In the article, the author uses non-technical language and explanations to describe the adaptability and intelligence of the crocodile. Identify at least three such examples and explain how each one helps the reader understand crocodiles. Use relevant and specific information from the article to support your answer.

_____

_____

_____

_____

_____

_____

_____

_____

_____

_____

_____

_____

_____

_____

37 Ⓐ Ⓑ Ⓒ Ⓓ

38 Ⓐ Ⓑ Ⓒ Ⓓ

39 Ⓐ Ⓑ Ⓒ Ⓓ

40 Ⓐ Ⓑ Ⓒ Ⓓ

Posttest Student Answer Booklet

GRADE 10
English Language Arts

COMPOSITION

_____

_____

_____

_____

_____

_____

_____

_____

_____

_____

_____

_____

_____

_____

_____

_____

_____

_____

_____

_____

POSTTEST ANSWER BOOKLET

Student's Name:

| LAST | | FIRST | | MI |

School: _____ Teacher: _____

Female ○   Male ○   Grade ⑨   ⑩   ⑪   ⑫

1 Ⓐ Ⓑ Ⓒ Ⓓ   **5** Ⓐ Ⓑ Ⓒ Ⓓ

2 Ⓐ Ⓑ Ⓒ Ⓓ   **6** Ⓐ Ⓑ Ⓒ Ⓓ

3 Ⓐ Ⓑ Ⓒ Ⓓ   **7** Ⓐ Ⓑ Ⓒ Ⓓ

4 Ⓐ Ⓑ Ⓒ Ⓓ   **8** Ⓐ Ⓑ Ⓒ Ⓓ

---

9 In the excerpt, the author describes Lilienthal's ideas, experiments, and accomplishments. Identify at least **three** character traits that Lilienthal demonstrated using relevant and specific information from the excerpt to support your answer.

_____

_____

_____

_____

_____

_____

_____

_____

_____

_____

10 Ⓐ Ⓑ Ⓒ Ⓓ

11 Ⓐ Ⓑ Ⓒ Ⓓ

12 Ⓐ Ⓑ Ⓒ Ⓓ

13 Ⓐ Ⓑ Ⓒ Ⓓ

14 Ⓐ Ⓑ Ⓒ Ⓓ

15 Ⓐ Ⓑ Ⓒ Ⓓ

16 Ⓐ Ⓑ Ⓒ Ⓓ

17 Ⓐ Ⓑ Ⓒ Ⓓ

18 Ⓐ Ⓑ Ⓒ Ⓓ

19 In the poem "After the Winter," the author frequently uses imagery to create mood. Identify at least **three** examples of imagery that convey mood in the second stanza of the poem. Use relevant and specific information from the poem to support your answer.

_____

_____

_____

_____

_____

_____

_____

_____

_____

_____

_____

_____

_____

_____

_____

20 Ⓐ Ⓑ Ⓒ Ⓓ

21 Ⓐ Ⓑ Ⓒ Ⓓ

22 Ⓐ Ⓑ Ⓒ Ⓓ

23 Ⓐ Ⓑ Ⓒ Ⓓ

24 Ⓐ Ⓑ Ⓒ Ⓓ

25 Ⓐ Ⓑ Ⓒ Ⓓ

26 Ⓐ Ⓑ Ⓒ Ⓓ

27 In this essay, Benjamin Franklin describes a terrible conflict he experienced with his brother. What was the conflict and how and when did it begin? Use details and information from the essay in your answer.

_____

_____

_____

_____

_____

_____

_____

_____

_____

_____

_____

_____

_____

_____

_____

28 Ⓐ Ⓑ Ⓒ Ⓓ

29 Ⓐ Ⓑ Ⓒ Ⓓ

30 Ⓐ Ⓑ Ⓒ Ⓓ

31 Ⓐ Ⓑ Ⓒ Ⓓ

32 Ⓐ Ⓑ Ⓒ Ⓓ

33 Ⓐ Ⓑ Ⓒ Ⓓ

34 Ⓐ Ⓑ Ⓒ Ⓓ

35 Ⓐ Ⓑ Ⓒ Ⓓ

36 This article mentions a type of storm called a hypercane. Why does the author discuss hypercanes? How might hypercanes be related to the extinction of the dinosaurs? Use details and information from the article in your answer.

_____

_____

_____

_____

_____

_____

_____

_____

_____

_____

_____

_____

_____

_____

_____

37 Ⓐ Ⓑ Ⓒ Ⓓ

38 Ⓐ Ⓑ Ⓒ Ⓓ

39 Ⓐ Ⓑ Ⓒ Ⓓ

40 Ⓐ Ⓑ Ⓒ Ⓓ